Urban Infrastructure:
Finance and Management

ORGANISATION FOR ECONOMIC CO-OPERATION AND DEVELOPMENT

Pursuant to Article 1 of the Convention signed in Paris on 14th December 1960, and which came into force on 30th September 1961, the Organisation for Economic Co-operation and Development (OECD) shall promote policies designed:

— to achieve the highest sustainable economic growth and employment and a rising standard of living in Member countries, while maintaining financial stability, and thus to contribute to the development of the world economy;
— to contribute to sound economic expansion in Member as well as non-member countries in the process of economic development; and
— to contribute to the expansion of world trade on a multilateral, non-discriminatory basis in accordance with international obligations.

The original Member countries of the OECD are Austria, Belgium, Canada, Denmark, France, Germany, Greece, Iceland, Ireland, Italy, Luxembourg, the Netherlands, Norway, Portugal, Spain, Sweden, Switzerland, Turkey, the United Kingdom and the United States. The following countries became Members subsequently through accession at the dates indicated hereafter: Japan (28th April 1964), Finland (28th January 1969), Australia (7th June 1971) and New Zealand (29th May 1973). The Commission of the European Communities takes part in the work of the OECD (Article 13 of the OECD Convention). Yugoslavia takes part in some of the work of the OECD (agreement of 28th October 1961).

Publié en français sous le titre :
INFRASTRUCTURES URBAINES :
Comment les financer?
Comment les gérer?

FOREWORD

This report was prepared by a Project Group established under the auspices of the OECD Group on Urban Affairs. It has been written by the OECD Urban Affairs Division, with the assistance of Professor Richard Kirwan (University Professor of Urban Economics and Consultant on urban affairs in Sydney, Australia). The report is the result of a two-year inquiry based on various case studies and national reports.

It deals mainly with "linear" urban infrastructure (i.e. water supply, sewerage, transport networks) and it considers management, financing, pricing and environmental issues. However, this report emphasizes mainly the financing and pricing mechanisms which can be used to deal with urban infrastructure provision, maintenance, repair and renewal, including the recourse to sophisticated public-private partnerships.

The OECD Group on Urban Affairs approved this report and endorsed its policy options at its 17th Session on 29 and 30 November 1990. The report is derestricted on the responsibility of the Secretary-General.

ALSO AVAILABLE

Cities and Transport (1988)
(97 88 09 1) ISBN 92-64-13183-3   FF210   £25.50   US$44.50   DM87

Environmental Policies for Cities in the 1990s (1990)
(97 90 03 1) ISBN 92-64-13435-2   FF100   £12.00   US$21.00   DM39

Managing and Financing Urban Services (1987)
(97 87 04 1) ISBN 92-64-12951-0   FF60   £6.00   US$11.00   DM22

Transport and the Environment (1988)
(97 88 01 1) ISBN 92-64-13045-4   FF95   £11.20   US$21.00   DM41

Cut along dotted line

ORDER FORM

Please enter my order for:

Qty.	Title	Price
....	....	....
....	....	....
....	....	....
....	....	....
		————
	Total :	....

- Payment is enclosed ☐
- Charge my VISA card ☐   Number of card ....
  (Note: You will be charged the French franc price.)
  Expiration of card .... Signature ....
- *Send invoice. A purchase order is attached* ☐

Send publications to *(please print):*

Name ....

Address ....

....

....

Send this Order Form to OECD Publications Service, 2, rue André-Pascal, 75775 PARIS CEDEX 16, France, or to OECD
Publications and Information Centre or Distributor in your country *(see last page of the book for addresses).*

Prices charged at the OECD Bookshop.

*THE OECD CATALOGUE OF PUBLICATIONS and supplements will be sent free of charge
on request addressed either to OECD Publications Service,
or to the OECD Distributor in your country.*

CONTENTS

SUMMARY AND POLICY OPTIONS

1. The challenge of providing urban infrastructure

In most OECD countries, the authorities responsible for managing and financing the provision of urban infrastructure face a number of challenges and constraints.

Urban economic restructuring

Cities remain the core of a massive process of economic restructuring, not only in old industrial areas, but also in more recently developed regions.

Ageing, obsolete, badly maintained infrastructure

In many cities, there is a need to replace or rehabilitate existing infrastructure, while at the same time there is a need to provide new infrastructure, better adapted to emerging industries and activities. Certain types of infrastructure and services have not coped well with urban change – e.g. transport; in the coming decade there is likely to be increasing pressure for a complete rethinking of their role, their form and their relationship with urban life.

Environmentally-friendly infrastructure

The urban environment is deteriorating and many categories of urban infrastructure need to be improved from the environmental point of view; a better quality of life for urban citizens, as well as an efficient use of national resources require more environmentally-friendly infrastructure.

The burden of cost

Total expenditure for urban infrastructure represent probably 3 to 5 per cent of the Gross Domestic Product (GDP). Investments in urban infrastructure constitute a significant element in total fixed capital formation – public and private. Those investments are still mainly provided by the public sector and they represent, together with the running cost of existing infrastructure, an important proportion of public budgets (national, regional and local). This in turn is focusing attention onto how the costs of urban infrastructure should be financed and who should bear them. The potential exists here for a successful conjuncture of user-pay and polluter-pay pricing systems.

Constraints on public expenditure

OECD countries face serious constraints on public expenditure and on public borrowing. The unwillingness of national and local authorities to increase their indebtedness severely limits the ways in which long-term investment in urban infrastructure can be financed.

Involving the private sector

The participation of private capital in the financing and management of urban infrastructure could relieve the public sector of the need to increase its debt.

2. The management of urban infrastructure in the public sector

Division of responsibilities

1. *There is a need to link closely investment decisions with maintenance responsibilities.* Capital works and programming, on the one hand, and maintenance and operations, on the other hand, need to be better integrated.

2. *The areas of political and professional responsibility should be demarcated clearly.* Undue interference between decision-makers and managers should be avoided; accountability of the providers of urban infrastructure should be improved and public participation in the design and operation of this infrastructure – especially when they have an impact on the environment – should be increased.

Improving the efficiency of public sector provision

3. *There is a need for performance targets, as well as for economic and financial targets.* Efficient management and effective use of available resources require that managers should have clear goals. Performance targets should directly reflect the objectives of public policy. New measures of performance may need to be established, together with improved mechanisms for monitoring the achievement of objectives. Economic and financial targets should be specified in terms of rates of return on capital used and assets (at current replacement valuation) and in the form of dividends payable, where appropriate.

4. *There is a need to develop incentives within the public sector.* Public infrastructure authorities tend to lack appropriate incentives to develop efficient investment and operational policies. Improved accounting methods and regular assessment of performance should be introduced and financial incentives should be established for managers, staff and workers.

5. *There is a need to introduce more competition.* Most urban infrastructures are still regarded as natural monopolies and the scope for competition remains therefore too limited. Even if privatisation is not desired, there are numerous ways in which the provision, the maintenance and the daily operation of urban public infrastructure services can be opened up to competition.

6. *There is a need to better respond to user preferences.* Public authorities which are responsible for urban infrastructure provision should establish a close "dialogue" with the users of this infrastructure. The corollary of a more competitive public sector provision of urban infrastructure is that public authorities need to become more sensitive to market demand. This will require closer liaison with customers and appropriate surveys to enquire about changing needs.

7. *There is a need to better account for the environmental impact of urban infrastructure.* The design and management of urban infrastructure should be

based on principles of environmental acceptability and sustainable development. The achievement of environmental objectives should become an integral part of infrastructure planning and operation (e.g. through environmental impact assessments). Existing urban infrastructure which is not environmentally satisfactory should be modified accordingly.

3. Financing and pricing in the public sector

Limitations on borrowing should encourage urban infrastructure providers to innovative ways of financing, such as the requirement for contributions by developers.

Pricing policy should be designed to enhance efficiency (by covering the costs of capital and operation and by internalising the environmental costs of urban infrastructure) and it should substantially contribute to the financing of urban infrastructure investments, maintenance, operation and renewal.

Financing

1. *Capital budgeting should be better adapted to the real cost of capital.* Where the real cost of capital is high, it is essential to economise on capital expenditures. This entails a continuing search for more efficient and less costly technical solutions and a better phasing of expenditures.

2. *At the same time there is a need to find a solution to the inflationary enhancement of nominal interest rates.* Three practical alternatives are:
   – *Inflation-indexed capital finance.* This is an efficient solution to inflation but it depends on the acceptability of indexed paper to the capital markets.
   – *Shifting the financing burden from current debt service to up-front capital contributions.* The great advantage of this approach is that it transfers to developers, land-owners or land-users the responsibility for recourse to the capital market.
   – *Equity financing.* This solution depends on, and constitutes a potential rationale for, greater private involvement in the financing of urban infrastructure.

3. *Wherever possible, urban infrastructure authorities should aim to derive a substantial part of their revenues from ear-marked streams (including benefit-related tax assessments) and their borrowings should be secured against future revenues.* Reliance on ear-marked revenues, as opposed to general taxation, will improve accountability and encourage efficiency. Securing borrowings against revenues will ensure that investment decisions are related to future needs.

4. *Accounting by infrastructure authorities should be based on replacement cost.* The accounting that underlies management decisions must be based on a full appreciation of the economic cost of the use of the resources involved, which can only be achieved through up-to-date replacement cost analysis. The cost of capital and the value of assets should automatically be adjusted for inflation.

Pricing

5. *Pricing of urban infrastructure should be designed to approximate to marginal cost pricing.* This approach achieves the greatest overall efficiency. It entails two

9

requirements: the use of an up-to-date analysis of replacement costs, appropriately depreciated, and a variation for significant peak loads and capacity constraints.

6. *All beneficiaries of urban infrastructure should contribute to its financing. User charges, linked with polluter charges, should be favoured.* The design of charging systems based on user charges should aim at the same time to incorporate pollution-related pricing mechanisms. This is particularly relevant in the case of water and sewage, as well as in the case of urban highways.

7. *Alternatives to direct user charges are up-front capital contributions (or charges) and beneficiary taxes.* The great merit of these approaches is that they are consistent with the policy objective of relating benefit to marginal cost, while at the same time they provide an up-front flow of funds that can reduce the need for public-sector borrowing in favour of urban infrastructure.

8. *Charges or taxes on urban development (or land values) that are intended to represent the price charged for new urban infrastructure should be distinguished from other taxes that may be used for general urban development purposes.* The aims of efficiency and equity require that general revenue-raising systems should not be mixed with the specific attempt to price urban infrastructure provision and maintenance.

9. *The distributional effects of pricing urban infrastructure should be taken into account.* A reasonable compromise between efficiency and inter-personal equity could be achieved by the use of basic entitlements or increasing block tariffs. Problems of inter-areal equity and inter-generational equity need also to be considered: for instance, it would not be equitable to load exclusively onto existing users of urban infrastructure the costs of providing capacity for the future.

4. Involving the private sector

General principles and forms of involvement

1. *The main objectives of involving private capital and management should be clearly established.* In the field of finance, the advantages of involving the private sector are the transfer of risk, substitutes for public borrowing and up-front costs, and the protection of present users and tax-payers from the burden of paying for future needs. In the field of management, the private sector has often more expertise than the public sector, more specific technical skills, more sophisticated budgeting and accounting techniques.

2. *There may be a need to design regulatory mechanisms prior to the involvement of the private sector.* The success of involving the private sector, the efficiency and equity of the result, will depend as much on the design of the regulatory framework as on the use of private capital itself.

3. *The form of private sector involvement should be selected according to specific objectives and local conditions.* Involving the private sector in the financing and management of urban infrastructure can take alternative forms:
   - specifically negotiated contributions;
   - joint public-private organisations;

- formal joint venturing;
- contracting out;
- granting of concessions;
- privatisation.

There is no single way of involving private capital and management expertise that is preferable in all circumstances. The choice of one of these forms of involvement will depend on local conditions and on the type of infrastructure considered.

Risks and prospects

4. **The capacity of the capital market to absorb the additional demand linked to the provision of a new urban infrastructure, and the risks entailed, need to be taken into account.** The successful involvement of private capital requires that the existing capacity and expertise of the private sector should be able to take on tasks which have generally been within the public sector. And in smaller economies such new tasks may entail capital inflow with undesirable consequences for the long-term balance of payments or level of foreign debt.

5. **The risks for the public sector of involving private capital and management should be assessed.** The corollary of transferring to the private sector the risks involved in investment in infrastructure is that they may prove too great for private capital to sustain, if economic conditions become adverse. The public sector must ensure that there are contingency plans and it must assess the likely extent of its own exposure.

6. **In case of joint public-private ventures, the true value of the public sector's initial equity must be assessed.** This may take the form of land or development rights or existing infrastructure, as well as the capture of existing revenues. Fair apportionment of the benefits of joint ventures depends on the design of schemes that are proof against changing economic conditions and that correctly reflect each party's initial investment.

5. Conclusions

Managing urban infrastructure

1. There is a need to develop appropriate structures for the day-to-day management and operation of urban infrastructure, and for longer-term strategic planning, with a view to encouraging efficiency.

2. There is a need to improve the incentives to efficiency and the level of competition in the public sector.

Financing and pricing

3. There is a need to adapt to the real cost of capital in ways that are efficient, equitable and environmentally acceptable.

4. There is a need to develop systems of beneficiary taxation and capital contributions to assist with the financing of infrastructure while preserving efficiency.

5. There is a need to develop pricing policies that will ensure efficient utilisation of urban infrastructure and assist with its financing.

Involving private sector capital and management

6. There is a need to specify clearly the reasons for involving the private sector; to distinguish between the benefits from access to private finance and from the transfer of management expertise; and to structure the arrangements that link the private sector to the provision of urban infrastructure accordingly.

7. There is a need to weigh the advantages and disadvantages of the different types of contractual arrangements between the public and the private sector.

8. There is a need to assess the consequences for public authorities of any loss of control and any exposure to risk that may be involved, and to develop appropriate means, including regulatory mechanisms, by which public authorities can continue to uphold the public interest.

Chapter 1

THE CONTEMPORARY CONTEXT: URBAN CHANGE AND ENVIRONMENTAL ADAPTATION

1. Introduction

In most OECD Member countries, the authorities responsible for managing and financing the provision of urban infrastructure face a difficult situation.

Urban conditions are changing: new demands are being placed on existing infrastructure. There is a growing recognition of the need to improve and review existing systems to bring them into line with present and future requirements. Meanwhile, in many countries, the demand for investment in new infrastructure remains strong.

Two issues are at the forefront of urban policy:
- the need to adapt and expand urban areas to meet the economic challenges and demands of the next century; and
- the need to reduce the harmful impacts of urban life on the environment and to develop environmentally-acceptable and sustainable forms of urban living.

Urban public infrastructure occupies a pivotal position in the search for ways of achieving both these objectives.

Efficient and productive cities depend on well-designed and economical infrastructure. As the composition of output and employment changes, and as growing incomes and changing demographic patterns create new demands for housing, leisure and other social needs, so the infrastructure of cities has to adapt.

The growing awareness of the need to reduce the harmful effects of urban life on the natural environment is imposing new requirements and new costs on the design and management of infrastructure.

Sustainable patterns of living and energy conservation are increasingly important determinants of the future form of urban development. Responsive policies for managing and providing urban infrastructure are urgently required.

13

2. The changing urban context

Restructuring for the urban future

Since the mid-1970s, there has been a shift (in most countries) away from manufacturing and primary production towards office-based activities (with a strong emphasis on finance) and personal and leisure-related services. This has been accompanied by a major restructuring of the economy and, in many cases, of the fabric of cities.

New investment in offices and tertiary-sector facilities, new approaches to the integration of manufacturing with the service sector (for example, in the case of business parks), the development of tourist-related facilities and leisure complexes and new patterns of retail trade have stimulated a large volume of new physical development in cities. The provision and renewal of the public infrastructure has not always kept pace. Behind these changes lie two important developments.

Forms of urban living

The first is in consumer preferences and the demand for urban living. Where the 1950s and 1960s were dominated, in many countries, by rapid growth in the demand for family housing, since the middle of the 1970s, the pattern of housing demand has swung clearly towards smaller households.

Especially in countries where family housing was strongly associated with the suburban peripheral development of cities, these developments have resulted in a marked shift in preferences in favour of more central locations.

In some ways, the move to smaller average household sizes has made it easier to provide adequate infrastructure. Existing facilities, like sewers and water mains, have been able to meet increases in demand due to redevelopment from the capacity released by falling household size. In fact an excess supply of some facilities, particularly social infrastructure like schools and hospitals, has emerged in many inner city areas.

But this has not wholly obviated the need to adapt existing infrastructure to new patterns of demand and to accommodate changes in the intensity of urban land use.

The changing structure of urban economic activity

The second driving force behind these developments has been the process of local economic restructuring. This has been manifest in most OECD countries since the mid-1970s. The shift towards tertiary activities, with especially strong growth in the finance and business services sectors, has been accompanied, in most countries, by a growing concentration of office development in the central areas of the larger cities.

At the same time the emphasis on fostering new sources of growth in manufacturing, especially in high-technology fields, has focused attention onto the differing needs and preferences of new branches of activity.

Airports have emerged as key components of the urban infrastructure which have a direct impact on the pace and location of activities.

Together, the effect of these changes has been to highlight three critical areas of urban policy and change:

- mobility and the capacity of urban transportation systems to accommodate the changing need and growing demand for the movement of people and goods within and between cities;
- environment and the need to reconcile developmental pressures with the requirement for environmentally-sustainable patterns of devclopment; and
- the emerging nexus between information flows (and the technology of communication), the use of leisure time and the cultural endowment of cities.

Cities in a competitive environment

During the 1980s, a strong underlying belief has emerged that competitive advantage in this process of restructuring – both between countries and between cities – depends very heavily on the ability of individual urban areas to offer a high quality of services and environment, well adapted to the needs of modern business and of its key employees.

Urban environment and urban services have been thrust to the forefront of the economic arena, in the struggle to attract foot-loose tertiary activities and high-technology industries. The quality of the environment and of basic infrastructure, as well as the provision of cultural and social facilities, are no longer viewed merely as objects of consumer demand or social concern but also as instruments of economic growth and survival.

The need to project an image appropriate to the times, to offer a high quality of life and environment, to provide infrastructure appropriate to emerging industries and new forms of development, both in concentrated agglomerations and low-density business parks, has given added stimulus to the search by city managers and local politicians to find new ways of meeting the need for urban infrastructure within increasingly tight budgets.

3. The environmental context

The 1980s have also been marked by a renewed awareness of the importance of environmental considerations in the development of economic activity.

The long-run maintenance of the natural environment is a public good. Ill-considered actions can have serious long-term costs. The principle is increasingly accepted that the costs of actions that destroy or pollute the environment should be put on those responsible.

The environmental impacts of urban life are a two-way process. Urban economic activities and patterns of living contribute to many forms of environmental degradation. But a good quality of environment is also highly valued by the households and businesses that choose to locate in cities[1].

Most types of urban infrastructure have a direct impact on the environment: surface water run-off can pollute surrounding water resources, as can the effluent from waste-water treatment processes; road transport facilities contribute to the pervading problem of atmospheric pollution, as well as to the degradation of living conditions; maintaining the quality of potable water supplies is a continuing concern.

There is a growing call for higher standards, affecting all categories of infrastructure. This is posing new problems for those charged with managing and providing infrastructure services. Inevitably it entails higher costs. And this in turn is focusing attention onto how those costs should be distributed.

Because of the long-term nature of many environmental problems issues of inter-generational equity have been brought to the forefront of debate.

4. Differences between countries

The problems of providing, managing and financing urban infrastructure are at their most acute in two different types of circumstance: where countries are experiencing areas of rapid or extensive new urbanisation; and where there is a need to upgrade existing or outworn infrastructure, often in the context of the redevelopment and maintenance of existing built-up areas.

Every country experiences both situations to some degree; but in most one or other predominates.

For example, in the more "mature" industrialised economies, like those of France, the United Kingdom and Belgium, the main problems faced by governments, national and local, are those associated with the redevelopment and maintenance of existing urban areas. In these countries the greater part of the infrastructure networks have been in place for many years.

In other countries, like Turkey, Australia and still to some extent Japan, whether due to rural-urban migration or to migration from overseas, the problem of providing infrastructure in areas of rapid new urbanisation is more critical.

No generalisation exactly fits all circumstances. In Japan, for example, the rate of urbanisation is slowing down and the issues connected with upgrading the quality of existing areas are becoming more important. In Australia there is evidence that an increasing proportion of funds will have to be devoted to the management and maintenance of existing infrastructure networks in the larger cities.

In Spain, as in some other countries, a period of rapid urbanisation has given way to a slower overall rate of urban growth, with more emphasis directed to the infrastructure needs of existing cities. So too in Sweden and Finland, the rate of urban expansion is much less rapid than it was in the 1960s and early 1970s.

In Italy, the evolving urban situation cannot be divorced from the continuing disparities in regional economic development and the related patterns of migration and government expenditure.

In France and the United Kingdom, despite much lower overall rates of new urbanisation, there remain areas where there is strong pressure for new urban development, carrying with it a need for appropriate additions to infrastructure.

The United States is an interesting case because it manifests both extremes of the situation. There is serious concern about the need for infrastructure renewal and replacement in the older cities, like New York, Boston and Chicago; while in other areas, notably southern California and Florida – to take just two examples – there remains a high rate of new urbanisation.

16

Canada also embraces areas of rapid development alongside areas where the pace of new urbanisation is much slower. However, the fastest rate of new urbanisation has been in some of the largest metropolitan areas.

Germany is also an interesting case. Though the age and structure of its cities points to the overriding importance of the management of infrastructure in existing built-up areas, the rate of population influx associated with political changes in eastern Europe is likely to result in a marked increase in future in the need for new urbanisation.

Chapter 2

A FRAMEWORK FOR MANAGEMENT AND POLICY INNOVATION

1. Definition of urban infrastructure

The infrastructure that is essential to the efficient working of a modern city is extensive. It includes provision for water and sewerage facilities, surface water drainage, highways, transport facilities, energy distribution networks, telecommunications facilities and other "networked" services. It also includes the provision of the types of social facilities which are regarded as essential to the maintenance of a tolerable standard of living for residents and workers: educational and health care facilities, leisure facilities and open space and the infrastructure associated with the maintenance of public health and welfare, law and order and public administration.

Within the compass of the work undertaken for this report it was not possible to cover all these different aspects of the provision of urban capital facilities. Different social and economic traditions in different countries in any event mean that practices are not always comparable.

For the purpose of this paper, therefore, a more limited focus has been adopted which is directed towards the main physical "networked" services. The components of urban public infrastructure discussed are therefore:
- water supply;
- sewerage networks;
- surface water drainage;
- highways, roads and associated facilities (such as bridges and tunnels); and
- public transport infrastructure.

2. The need for new initiatives

The challenge for urban infrastructure authorities is acute.

In many larger and older cities, substantial parts of the basic infrastructure were first constructed as much as (or more than) a century ago. While there is no evidence that wholesale replacement is imminent, the incidence of structural failure and the need for renewal and maintenance expenditure is growing. Even more recently built infrastructure is showing signs of strain. Infrastructure systems are being used much more intensively than they are being renewed; the result is widespread economic depreciation and impending obsolescence. Many infrastructure networks are being called on to meet demands for which they were not designed.

Urban highways, no less than inter-urban networks, are experiencing increasing damage from the high axle loads of modern freight transport and increasing volumes of traffic. Water and sewer systems are expected to satisfy increasingly stringent environmental criteria, as evidence emerges of the cumulative damage caused to the environment by inadequate protective measures. Many urban sewer systems face increasing problems from the discharge of toxic wastes by local industry. Households and businesses expect higher levels of protection against flood and storm damage. Meanwhile the strong growth of Central Business Districts in recent years, fuelled by the structural shift to financial, producer and cultural services, has in many cases increased (or renewed) the peak-load demand for public transportation.

At the same time, in a number of countries recent economic growth combined with changing social and demographic patterns is continuing to stimulate a high level of demand for housing. Much of this has to be satisfied in areas of new urbanisation where as a consequence there is a strong demand for the rapid provision of a high standard of infrastructure. In addition, there remain in many countries relatively underprivileged areas and communities where a backlog of infrastructure deficiencies needs to be made good[2].

The difficulties should not be exaggerated. The provision of urban public infrastructure has always been problematic. Investment in relatively expensive, long-lasting and often "lumpy" capital works in advance of need, well timed and well located, has always been, and remains, one of the major problems of modern urbanisation. Moreover, in a number of countries, including the United States, Canada and Japan, an upturn in expenditure on urban infrastructure during the 1980s suggests that an attempt is being made to redress the balance. The problem may indeed be more one of an inappropriate allocation of resources than of a need for substantial additional funding[3]. But in important ways the current situation remains different from those of previous decades.

3. Challenges for the future

Against this background, the national and sub-national authorities responsible for the provision and management of urban infrastructure must confront a number of issues:

Physical condition

First, there is the growing problem of maintaining and reviewing older infrastructure. Age itself is not always a good guide to the need for renewal. Nonetheless, the combination of age-related deterioration, of pressure from the new and growing demands and of adverse geo-physical conditions is a legitimate cause of anxiety in parts of many cities.

Exactly because much infrastructure is long-lasting and (like sewerage and water supply, for example) for long periods requires relatively little outlay on maintenance or renewal, many communities are lulled into a false sense of permanence. Facing up to the needs of an ageing infrastructure requires new approaches, new attitudes and above all a new awareness.

It requires estimation of the true rate of capital consumption; the design and implementation of appropriate pricing policies; the optimisation of maintenance and renewal programmes; a search for new technologies; new managerial and institutional structures; and above all cogent political articulation of the justification for expenditures.

Environment

Second, there is the environmental dimension.

The renewed concern world-wide about the environmental impact of urban life has placed onerous new requirements onto the providers and managers of urban infrastructure. Standards which once were acceptable are no longer so.

For example, water supply and waste water treatment plants have to meet increasingly high standards. Local populations are less willing to tolerate the noise and pollution generated by high-capacity highways. In some areas these are not difficult to achieve. But in others, whether because of past neglect or for intrinsic geographical reasons, the costs are high.

The need for additional expenditure to raise the standards of existing infrastructure or to construct new high-quality facilities highlights the question who should pay and how such expenditures should be financed. The potential exists for a successful conjuncture of user-based and pollution-related pricing systems.

Cost of capital and land

Third, there is the problem of inflation and the high cost of capital. Investment in long-lasting facilities is intrinsically difficult when the cost of capital is high. Financing mechanisms are not well adapted to spreading the burden of cost.

This too requires appropriate adaptations: new approaches to programming investment, new technical solutions, new financing mechanisms. So long as it falls to the public sector to provide most of the basic infrastructure that makes modern urban life economically and socially viable, public authorities cannot escape the need for innovation.

The high cost of land is an added problem in some countries, notably Japan, where it is a major constraint on programmes for improving and providing new infrastructure, especially in existing urbanised areas. In some countries there are problems about land acquisition and compensation arrangements. Community resistance to the use of land for infrastructure, mainly in already-occupied areas, is also a wide-spread problem.

Public expenditure restraints

Fourth, there is the overriding need, accepted in most OECD countries, to restrain public expenditure and public borrowing for reasons of macroeconomic policy.

This has had the effect both of stimulating the search for ways of transferring at least part of the burden of cost to private funding and of focusing attention onto the real return to expenditures on urban infrastructure. And this in turn requires that infrastructure should be used efficiently and, where possible, priced appropriately. The macroeconomic imperative entails microeconomic adjustment: public sector efficiency is an issue of increasing significance.

Equity

Finally, running throughout the emerging agenda, there is a wide-spread concern with maintaining fair and equitable access to urban infrastructure (and related services) at a time when the force of economic change is tending to widen the gap between the fortunes of the "haves" and the "have-nots" within and between urban areas.

Because of the long-term character of much infrastructure investment and the complexity of many of the environmental issues involved, questions of inter-generational equity are also of fundamental importance.

4. The context for improved decisions

The traditional structures for providing and managing infrastructure within the public sector have shown themselves in many countries to be slow to adapt to new requirements and to lack incentives to efficiency. In part the blame lies with the political processes that impose on public sector managers constraints and interference which distract them from the simpler goals faced by their private sector counterparts.

But the problems are often also ones of scale, of organisational structure and of the underlying "culture" of public sector management which rates efficiency alongside other objectives as only one of a number of concerns.

In some countries, a lack of information about the true state of much urban infrastructure hampers sound economic planning. During the last decade, a serious effort has been made to improve local information bases. New technologies – for example, different types of remote sensing and inspection equipment – have played an important role in this process. But information can only be improved at a cost; and this is often high. The costs and benefits of system-wide information have to be considered carefully.

There remains a need for better measures of performance and for indicators of the efficiency with which existing urban infrastructure is satisfying the needs and demands for which it has been provided.

The management of infrastructure and the formulation of policy raise wide-ranging issues that call for careful evaluation: issues of efficiency, of distributive justice, of environmental acceptability. Public participation and thorough discussion are essential to good decision-taking. Efficiency cannot be assessed only in terms of outcomes: the process by which decisions are arrived at is an important and potentially valuable component of the whole.

As a recent United Kingdom study has reiterated, a sound approach to management and policy requires five elements:

- clear identification of objectives and of the problems that are directly relevant to them;
- establishment of options, in the context of wide-spread consultation and debate;
- technical forecasts of future demands and costs;

- economic and financial evaluation; and
- assessment of environmental and social impacts[4].

In this context, the management of infrastructure requires a broad range of inputs, including: an understanding of urban change and urban planning, through analysis of environmental impacts, sensitivity to social problems and community attitudes and rigorous economic and financial appraisal.

5. Focus of the report

The focus of this report is more limited. The intention has been to concentrate on two subjects of growing interest and concern:
- the organisation and structure of the management of urban infrastructure (and related services); and
- the financing of capital and current expenditure.

These two areas were chosen both because the underlying problems appeared to be matters of growing concern in a wide range of OECD Member countries and because there exists a substantial body of experience in relation to innovation and managerial developments on which to draw.

Throughout the OECD countries there is in fact increasing recognition of the need and scope for innovation in the context of the overall search for ways of improving the efficiency and responsiveness of public sector management and the diversification of ways of funding public infrastructure.

At the technical and managerial level, there is a need for new ways of relating expenditure decisions to the returns that they are expected to generate. There is a need for better estimates of capital consumption and of past depreciation; for improved ways of optimising maintenance and replacement expenditures; for programming methods that better reflect budget constraints and the cost of capital. There is a need for new technical solutions and engineering designs, that exploit present-day technologies and better reflect current economic costs, financing methods and the changing balance between maintenance and investment needs.

Finally there is a need for new management structures with the right organisational characteristics and incentives to develop appropriate policies for the future.

At the level of policy, there is a clear need to reassess the ways in which urban infrastructure is allocated and priced, both to see whether it can be utilised more efficiently and to relate its use more effectively to the rate of capital consumption. There is a need to determine the real contribution of urban infrastructure to the economy, both local and national. And there is a need to explore new ways of financing the expenditures that will be required in future.

These concerns therefore form the main focus of this report.

Chapter 3

STRUCTURAL REFORM AND THE SEARCH FOR EFFICIENT AND EFFECTIVE SYSTEMS

1. The need for reform in the public sector

Throughout the 1980s the main emphasis of economic policy in a wide range of OECD countries has been on controlling and reducing public expenditure and borrowing.

This has formed the background to the problems faced by sub-national public authorities with responsibility for urban public infrastructure. Revenues have not been increasing fast enough to support expenditure programmes. Borrowing has been restricted. And the high cost of capital has made it impossible to finance investment out of limited revenues and created a short-term cash-flow "gap" between debt-service charges and actual or potential revenues.

More recently, however, the emphasis of national economic policies has swung more towards the need for microeconomic or structural reform, particularly but not exclusively of public sector activities. This has not replaced the concern with overall fiscal restraint; but it is an added focus of attention.

The need for structural reform is a logical product of the additional constraints that have been placed on public budgets: it is more than ever imperative that the maximum benefit should be derived from the expenditures and investments which the public sector can sustain, especially in areas where there is no substitute for public involvement. While it is often reasonable to assume an adequate level of efficiency in the private sector if certain well known conditions are satisfied – for example, adequate information, incentives and competition, backed up by sanctions for failure – there is no equivalent basis for presuming efficiency in the public sector.

It is generally recognised that there are two types of efficiency: allocative efficiency and productive efficiency.

Allocative efficiency requires that resources are allocated to producing the right goods and services in the right quantities. Information gathered from those to whom the expenditures are directed, equivalent to the signals that private producers derive from their revenues and marketing, is an essential input to the process of achieving allocative efficiency.

In this regard, many public authorities are developing increasingly sophisticated surveys and choice models. But there is also a significant role for collective decision-taking in relation to publicly-provided goods and services. Getting the balance right is not easy.

Productive efficiency is more straightforward. It requires only that the goods and services provided should be provided at the least cost and the highest standard that is consistent with the amount of resources available. This certainly should be an objective of any programme of public expenditure.

2. Some sources of efficiency and inefficiency

The main objective of structural reform in the public sector is to increase productivity.

Overall productivity in many branches of the public sector is hard to measure. Nonetheless, it has become increasingly common for governments to require evidence of productivity gains before authorising wage and salary increases for public sector workers.

In the field of infrastructure, the problems of measurement are more straightforward. There is substantial scope for increasing productivity, not least when the cost of services, or constituent elements, is manifestly higher than the cost of equivalent activities in the private sector.

Recent debate has centered on three issues for improving efficiency in the public sector:

Objectives

The need for improved specification of the objectives of public sector programmes has been recognised for some time. But previous attempts to formalise this – for example, through the application of so-called "planning and programming budget systems" (PPBS) – have not generally been successful. In many countries they have been abandoned. There remains a need for improved specification of objectives and improved measurement of outcomes.

Improved analysis of impacts

The public sector lacks adequate information about the impacts of its programmes. This hampers the development of new programmes. *Ex post* evaluation of past expenditures is still the exception rather than the rule. Where private enterprises must live with the product of their decisions – revenues either exceed or fall short of expectations – in the public sector all too often attention is primarily focused on the decision itself, especially when it is an object of intense controversy: managerial concern with actual outcomes easily wanes.

Incentives

The lack of a simple objective in the public sector, equivalent to maximising the return on shareholders' funds in the private sector, flows through to the lack of clear incentives for public sector managers and organisations to perform as efficiently as possible. It is doubtful if any simple equivalent could be devised. But incentives are needed.

The private sector offers a model, albeit not easily transferable to the circumstances of the public sector. It can be argued, for example, that, at least in the recent past, the incentives and criteria applied in the private sector have tended to emphasize short-run gains at the expense of long-run achievement. This would be undesirable in relation to urban infrastructure; for although it is necessary for infrastructure programmes to fit in with the short-run economic realities of constrained budgets, high interest rates and so on, infrastructure remains in essence a long-run investment to which long-run criteria are applicable.

The aim of structural reform should be to apply to the management of public sector services and investment the best and most relevant practices prevalent in the private sector.

In the private sector competition constitutes the most significant continuous spur to improving productivity.

The benefits of competition do not depend only on the existence of multiple producers. As Baumol et al have pointed out[5], the critical requirement is that monopoly can be contested. Even where this is unrealistic, either because existing monopoly suppliers have entrenched advantages or because they can successfully exclude potential competitors, it is still possible to introduce market signals into parts of the process of public sector provision.

In recent years increasing attempts have been made to open up components of public sector programmes to competitive bidding. Examples include the procurement of supplies and the provision of specific services. Various methods are increasingly employed, including open tendering and the contracting out of specific activities.

Preliminary studies suggest that this has been successful in keeping down costs and has not entailed a reduction in standards.

3. The challenge for urban infrastructure

Two main tasks that face those responsible for urban infrastructure are thus:
- finding ways of financing the continued provision and maintenance of urban infra-structure in the face of increasingly constrained budgets, restrictions on borrowing and limitations on increases of revenues; and
- improving the efficiency of the management of urban infrastructure and related services.

Recent experience in OECD countries reveals a variety of different approaches to these two imperatives.

Some relate only to managerial initiatives, some to innovative measures of financing; some intrinsically combine the two.

At the same time there are examples of initiatives wholly within the public sector; and examples that involve drawing in, in varying measure, private sector managerial expertise and private capital.

Developments in the management and organisation of urban infrastructure within the public sector are considered in Chapter 5.

Developments in financing and pricing, also within the public sector, are outlined in Chapter 6.

The different ways of involving private management and capital are considered in Chapter 7.

First, however, in the following chapter, the overall economic significance of urban infrastructure is reviewed (Chapter 4).

ECONOMIC SIGNIFICANCE OF URBAN INFRASTRUCTURE

1. The economic significance of expenditures on urban infrastructure

There is a serious dearth of aggregated information about expenditure on urban public infrastructure.

In most countries much of the responsibility for urban infrastructure rests with local bodies. The relevant information is not centralised. National statistical agencies maintain estimates of the overall levels of capital and current expenditure. But they rarely distinguish urban from non-urban expenditures.

Participating Member countries were invited to supply information as the basis for an analysis of the economic significance of urban infrastructure investment and current spending. In the event figures are only available for seven countries and even for these the information available is very limited.

The context is provided by the split between current and capital expenditures within overall national economic output and the division of each of these two between public and private activity.

There is broad similarity between the European countries and Canada in the ratio between Gross Domestic Product and Gross Fixed Capital Formation, though in the European countries there is evidence of a slight reduction in the proportion of available resources devoted to capital formation. In the United States the ratio is somewhat lower. The one outstanding exception is Japan, where proportionately almost a half as much again is devoted to capital formation.

These changes are illustrated by the figures in Table 1.

In absolute terms it is also notable that only in Japan has there been a marked increase in Gross Fixed Capital Formation (at constant prices) over the period 1980-87. Expenditure is also up in the United Kingdom, Canada and the United States but has been level in France and Germany.

The relative contributions of the public and private sectors to national capital formation differ markedly from one country to another. In Sweden, the share of the private sector is notably small – only a little over one half – while in Germany, France and Canada, the public sector share is only slightly over 10 per cent. In Japan, the public sector is responsible for about one-quarter of the total, while in the United States the public sector contribution fell as low as 6.5 per cent in 1985.

Table 1. **Gross fixed capital formation**

	1980	1987
Gross Fixed Capital Formation as per cent of GDP		
Canada	21.2	22.8
France	21.7	19.4
Germany	22.9	20.6
Japan	31.4	29.3
Sweden	20.2	19.9
United Kingdom	19.9	20.5
United States	17.9	18.1[1]
Private sector as per cent of Gross Fixed Capital Formation		
Canada	88.3	88.9
France	86.6	83.7
Germany	85.1	87.8
Japan	72.3	76.8
Sweden	55.7	[2]
United Kingdom	71.8	84.4
United States	92.0	93.5[1]

1. 1985.
2. Figures not available.

The most notable development revealed by the survey, however, is the very large increase in the share of the private sector in the United Kingdom over the period, from 72 per cent in 1980 to 84 per cent in 1987.

It is also notable that in all the countries for which figures are available, with the exception of the United Kingdom, there was a reduction in the percentage of capital formation devoted to infrastructure over the period 1980 to 1987. The relative fall was particularly marked in the case of the United States (Table 2). This probably reflects the resurgence of investment in industry. In the United Kingdom the rise in the proportion of infrastructure investment was associated with a significant increase in investment in highways, as well as water and sewerage.

In relative terms, however, there was a small shift away from water and sewerage investment in the United Kingdom over the period (Table 3). Similar shifts were experienced also in Canada, France and Sweden, in the latter case the shift also benefiting public transport investment. In Germany the most notable change in the composition of infrastructure investment was also away from highways in favour of public transport. This shift probably reflects the concern with stimulating economic growth which dominated the early part of the 1980s.

The figures provided by five countries reveal markedly different situations in relation to the division of responsibility for infrastructure between the public and private sectors. (No comparable information is available for Japan or the United Kingdom).

As might be expected, the countries in which overall the private sector plays the most significant role in relation to Gross Fixed Capital Formation – the United States and

Table 2. Capital investment in infrastructure

	1980	1987
Physical infrastructure investment[1] *as per cent of Gross Fixed* *Capital Formation*		
Canada	8.7	5.9
France	7.1	6.7
Germany	10.4	8.8[2]
Japan	[3]	[3]
Sweden	[3]	[3]
United Kingdom	3.8	4.6
United States	11.7	13.7[4]

1. Water, sewerage, drainage, highways and public transport (including railways).
2. 1986 figure on 1987 GDP base.
3. Figures not available.
4. 1985.

Table 3. Composition of investment in physical infrastructure[1]

As per cent of total

	Water supply	Sewerage	Surface drainage	Highways	Public transport
Canada					
1980	19.9	10.5	2.9	54.3	12.5
1987	17.9	8.6	2.9	56.9	13.8
France					
1980	9.8	14.6	3.7	46.1	25.8
1987	6.3	12.5	2.8	53.8	24.5
Germany					
1980	9.5	22.0	2.2	48.5	17.8
1986[2]	9.0	22.2	1.4	45.4	22.3
Sweden					
1980[3]					
1987	10.0	14.8	15.2	48.5	11.5
United Kingdom					
1980	15.1	18.1	4.4	53.3	9.9
1987	13.0	14.5	2.0	59.8	10.7
United States					
1980	23.1	18.3	[4]	44.1	14.6
1985[2]	23.1	18.3	[4]	44.0	14.6

1. Water, sewerage, drainage, highways, public transport (including railways).
2. 1987 figures not available.
3. Figures not available.
4. Included under water supply.

31

Canada – a major share of infrastructure investment is attributed to the private sector (over 50 per cent in the case of the United States, and more than two-fifths in the case of Canada).

In Sweden where Gross Fixed Capital Formation is dominated by the public sector, no infrastructure investment is undertaken by the private sector.

In France the greater part of investments in infrastructure are undertaken by the public sector. However, France is at the same time one of the countries in OECD where the management of infrastructure and infrastructure services is most commonly undertaken by joint public-private bodies or by private companies. The divergence arises from the dominant contractual relationship employed, namely the "farming out" of responsibility or concessions (Chapter 7).

In Germany despite the high overall percentage of Gross Fixed Capital Formation undertaken by the private sector, its contribution to infrastructure investment is miniscule: less than 1 per cent.

Only one country – Japan – was able to provide figures relating to the distribution of investment between urban areas. However, the proportions relate only to the incomplete figures which are available of total investment in physical infrastructure. They suggest that the split in 1987 was between slightly over four-fifths of investment in smaller urban areas and slightly under two-fifths in the three large metropolitan areas (Tokyo, Osaka and Nagoya). But the proportion flowing to the larger areas has been increasing.

Only Canada and the United States were able to provide full information about investment in infrastructure and about the size of the existing capital stock and the rate of capital consumption. The figures for Canada reveal a rate of investment well in excess of the rate of capital consumption – in 1987 the ratio was 1.73 – and annual investment equal to nearly 8 per cent of the value of the stock. However, the figures do suggest that these rates have fallen over the period: the equivalent figures for 1980 being 2.04 and 8.9 per cent.

In the United States, by contrast, the ratio of new capital formation to capital consumption was only 1.48 in 1980 and 1.11 in 1985. Annual investment in 1980 and 1985 was equivalent to 7.9 and 7.4 per cent of the value of the current capital stock respectively, reflecting the relative reduction in investment in physical infrastructure over the period.

However, the remaining useful life of the stock of physical infrastructure in the United States is estimated to have increased from 12.8 to 14.5 years between 1980 and 1985. Current investment in each year therefore also exceeded the rate of depreciation (net asset value divided by remaining useful life) despite the decline (at constant prices) in the overall level of investment.

It is difficult to draw general conclusions from this analysis, both because of the small number of countries represented in the sample and because of the inadequacy of much of the data. It is particularly difficult that national governments do not by and large maintain statistical records which would allow the separate identification of trends relating to urban, as opposed to non-urban, areas or to categories of urban areas, such as the major cities and metropolitan centres.

In the absence of this information we can only hazard a guess as to the real significance of urban public infrastructure investment in the context of overall expenditure patterns. In countries which are generally highly urbanised, however, it is clear that investment in the major categories of physical infrastructure – water and sewerage, surface drainage, highways and public transport facilities – constitutes a significant element in total fixed capital formation and one which deserves to be given more attention.

2. Public infrastructure investment and macroeconomic policy

It is generally accepted that the control of public expenditure (or its rate of increase), and more specifically the control of public borrowing, are essential to the macroeconomic management of the economy. Urban infrastructure investment is typically the responsibility of lower-levels of government (or equivalent authorities), though subventions of varying magnitudes are often available from higher levels of government (especially for transportation and water storage projects).

Whether or not urban infrastructure investment specifically "crowds out" private investment or expenditure is debatable. The argument is usually pursued as a general one in relation to the role and effects of public expenditure and borrowing. However, a more detailed study by Aschauer of the relationship between public investment and private spending in the United States over the period 1953 to 1984 tends to confirm the view that public investment is a direct substitute for private investment[6].

In a Canadian study by Sonnen and Haney of the macroeconomic impact of spending on infrastructure, reported in more detail below, the authors assumed that some crowding out was inevitable, unless funds were wholly borrowed overseas[7].

Private investment in infrastructure may also affect the capital market. Competitors in the bid for the Channel Tunnel concession were discouraged from raising a major block of funds exclusively on the London capital market for fear of the effect it might have on the cost of capital.

The extent to which investment in infrastructure, or expenditures on operations and maintenance, can be restrained for reasons of macroeconomic policy varies from country to country in accordance with different constitutional and budgetary practices. The most common types of control are over total public spending or public borrowing. Australia and the United Kingdom provide contemporary examples of this type of restraint being imposed by national governments. At issue in many cases is whether or not the expenditures of semi-public or para-statal autonomous authorities fall within the ambit of control.

Controls may also be imposed on the level, or more typically the rate of increase, of related taxes or charges: for example, their increase is often pegged to, or below, the rate of inflation. Since the "tax-payers' revolt" of the late 1970s in the United States, this type of control has been wide-spread at the sub-national level. For example, most Australian States similarly limit the rate of increase of local taxes and similar charges.

The effect of all such controls is to limit the provision of urban infrastructure irrespective of the rate of return it might generate.

Controls exercised from above can be distinguished from the fiscal discipline imposed by authorities themselves or by more local tiers of government in response to the emerging economic conditions. This too tends to take the form of a limit on the rate of increase of taxes or charges.

The effect of such controls has been twofold: to focus attention onto the contribution made by urban infrastructure to national and regional productivity and growth; and to encourage a search for financing mechanisms that are exempt from control. It is difficult to find ways around controls that limit revenues, though legal differentiation between categories of revenue – for example, between taxes and charges – may leave some scope for evading specific controls. It is generally easier to devise methods of financing infrastructure that overcome restrictions on public spending or borrowing.

On the other hand, it is rare these days to find examples where investment in urban infrastructure is being encouraged on macroeconomic grounds. The outstanding example at the present time is Japan, though there remain places in a number of countries – often at sub-national levels of government – where public investment is still regarded as an appropriate stimulative or counter-cyclical device. In Japan, the main argument in favour of increasing investment in urban infrastructure has been to stimulate domestic demand. This is seen to be a necessary counter-balance to the continuing balance-of-payments surplus. Since urban infrastructure investment has in the past been somewhat neglected in Japan, in favour of other categories of capital formation, it seems unlikely that this policy implies an unacceptable fall in the real rate of return on investment at the margin.

3. The economic role of urban infrastructure

Two approaches have been adopted to exploring the relationship between public spending on infrastructure and economic growth or productivity. The first one focuses on the relationship between infrastructure provision and the economic performance of individual enterprises; the other is pitched at an aggregate level of analysis[8].

Microeconomic analysis of the productivity of individual enterprises identifies the first-round components of the relationship between infrastructure and growth, but tends to ignore secondary and spill-over effects.

Many local studies have been undertaken to demonstrate the need for specific infrastructure works to enable plants, especially in the manufacturing sector, to work to maximum efficiency. Typical requirements include improved access to the highway system, adequate water supplies and appropriate systems for the discharge of effluent waste. Studies at this level, however, tend not to identify the relationship between the enterprise's efficiency and broader characteristics of the infrastructure system. A good example in this regard is the overall state of the urban transportation system. It is generally true that transport costs are not a large element in most manufacturing firms' total costs these days. Location and relocation decisions, moreover, are likely to be motivated predominantly by the need for more space (for new forms of plant lay-out and for future expansion).

Nonetheless, it remains true that firms are sensitive to the advantages of locations with good general accessibility characteristics for the movement of goods within and between urban areas. Similarly the more labour-intensive activities, especially in the tertiary sector, are strongly influenced by the availability of transport for employees. At this level urban transportation infrastructure clearly remains an important element in the overall efficiency of a business; but it is not easy to turn this into an aggregate estimate of the potential return to increased investment in urban transport facilities.

In practice, the overall effect on business profitability of variations in the quality and availability of infrastructure is unlikely to be large, since consequential variations in land rents or prices act to offset the gains or losses due to more or less well-provided locations. Spatial pricing (through the cost of sites) compensates for inaccessibility and the lack of publicly-provided infrastructure, after taking into account the taxes or charges payable.

A recent study in the United Kingdom by Diamond and Spence of the relationship between infrastructure and industrial costs relies on direct survey data. It reports considerable dissatisfaction among the firms surveyed with the state of the infrastructure in the United Kingdom. But its conclusions relate predominantly to national infrastructure systems and not to specifically urban infrastructure[9].

The second approach to this question has attempted to identify the relationship between infrastructure provision and productivity through aggregate analysis.

It is often asserted that there is an important relationship between the level of public investment and the rate of growth of the economy[10]. Unfortunately there are not many examples of rigorous attempts to establish the relationship, few that are spatially disaggregated and still fewer that highlight specifically the role of urban public infrastructure.

During the 1970s, Mera attempted to establish a relationship between regional productivity and the stock of public capital in Japan and the United States. From his study of regional data for Japan over the period 1954-63, he concluded that social capital had a marginal productivity not dissimilar to private capital. From his analysis of the United States regions over the period 1947-63, he concluded that the growth of public infrastructure was a major cause of the more rapid growth of some regions than others. In the case of Japan it should be noted that the historical endowment of social capital at the time studied was not high. This might have had the effect of increasing its marginal productivity. In the case of the United States it is worth noting that the period studied by Mera was one during which public expenditure and capital formation grew rapidly[11].

Since then there have been a number of attempts to explore the interrelationship further in the United States. The results, however, are not always consistent or easy to interpret.

Hulten and Schwab analysed regional productivity growth in the manufacturing sector over the period 1951-78. They concluded that overall the contribution of the volume of capital to the growth of output was small, compared to the growth of total factor productivity; but they found that differences between regions in the volume of capital input were more significant in accounting for regional differences in the growth of output[12].

Aschauer undertook an analysis of the relationship between public consumption and investment, private investment and the rate of return on private capital over the period 1953-84. He concluded that the level of public capital "strongly influences the net return to private capital" and that "the public capital stock appears to be too low." This is because there is a significant difference in the marginal return to investment in the two sectors[13].

Eberts studied data for 40 cities over the period 1904-78 and concluded that in older cities public investment was likely to lead private investment, whereas in more recently-growing cities private investment occurred first, leaving public investment to catch up later[14]. Subsequently, Eberts analysed data for 38 cities over the twenty-year period from 1958 to 1978. From this study he concluded that while public and private capital are in general substitutes, public investment turns out to be complementary to manufacturing employment in the regional production function: i.e. public capital spending is necessary to the growth of manufacturing. But "the overall effect ... on manufacturing output is relatively small"[15].

A recent review of the relationship between transport investment and local economic development in the United Kingdom, by Grieco[16], concludes: "The case for investment in transport as a stimulus to economic growth has not yet been established; at the general level it remains unproven that transport investment raises the overall level of national economic activity. At the local level, it has not yet been widely researched ...". Hall and Hass-Klau, drawing on evidence from Germany and the United Kingdom, were similarly pessimistic about the link in the relation to public transportation[17].

Chapter 5

THE ORGANISATION AND MANAGEMENT OF INFRASTRUCTURE IN THE PUBLIC SECTOR

1. Traditional arrangements

In most OECD countries the responsibility for urban infrastructure rests with public authorities; but the division of responsibility between levels of government and between government and semi-government, or independent, authorities varies from country to country.

This section briefly reviews these traditional arrangements.

In Spain, legal responsibility for the water supply system and for sewers and drains rests with municipalities. However, the actual supply is often organised through separate companies. Private companies have been supplying water in some cities, large and small, for example Barcelona, for more than a century.

In the case of Madrid water supply and sewerage are provided by an autonomous publicly-owned company, the *Canal de Isabel II.*

Highways within urban boundaries are the responsibility of municipalities, which also operate the rapid transit ("metro") systems. But rail transport otherwise is the responsibility of the national railway company.

In central and northern Italy urban infrastructure services are mainly provided by autonomous public enterprises. In southern Italy, however, there are few specialised units capable of taking responsibility for the delivery and financing of these services. These are mainly the direct responsibility of regional and local governments. As a consequence there is much greater political involvement in the decision process – for example, the setting of charges – in the south.

In Canada, responsibility for infrastructure is mainly divided between the local, regional and provincial levels of government, although the Federal government also has a role. Municipalities are the operating authority for most categories of infrastructure. However, the regional tier of government – which exists in most large metropolitan areas in addition to local government – has responsibility for planning and for capital budgeting in relation to urban infrastructure.

The provincial level of government is also involved through funding initiatives and controls over standards; it is also usually responsible for major urban transportation and transit facilities. While the Federal government has had funding programmes for urban sewer and water systems, grade separation of highways and the Trans-Canada Highway network, its activities in relation to urban infrastructure are now principally limited to environmental research.

In Finland, once again it is municipalities that have the primary responsibility for urban highways and water and sewerage. However, in the smaller communities, there exist private water and sewerage facilities, whose operations are regulated by the municipality.

In France, although ultimate responsibility is vested in local communes, municipalities often co-operate through "supra-local" bodies to provide infrastructure and related services. The form and extent of this co-operation is very variable. But the practice is extensive: for example, two-thirds of all local communes participate in some joint arrangement for water supply and distribution.

Responsibility for managing and operating infrastructure systems is commonly delegated to semi-public or private bodies. For example, about 70 per cent of the water supply network (in terms of population served) and a slightly smaller proportion of the sewerage system is subject to some form of delegation or concession. Almost all local public transport services are similarly contracted out.

In Japan, responsibility for urban sewers and drainage schemes is split between the municipal and prefectural levels of government. Municipalities are responsible for local sewer networks and for urban storm-water drains, while the prefectural level is typically responsible for larger areas schemes that conform to a "river basin" or catchment area.

Highways in Japan are divided between municipal, prefectural and national control, though in some instances the construction and maintenance of major roads within urban areas is undertaken by regional public corporations or corporations established by the national government specifically for the purpose – e.g. the Japan Highway Public Corporation or the Metropolitan Expressway Public Corporation.

Many rail-based rapid transit systems in Japan, however, are privately owned and operated.

In the United Kingdom, responsibility for water and sewerage was until very recently vested in ten regional authorities, which together with 30 smaller licenced private companies, provided water and sewerage services throughout England and Wales. Local councils acted as their agents in providing and maintaining the sewerage system. In Scotland, however, the responsibility lies directly with the regional tier of government, for which there is no equivalent in England and Wales.

At the end of 1989 responsibility for water and sewerage in England and Wales was transferred to ten public limited companies and privatised. This is discussed further in Chapter 7 of this report. In the larger metropolitan areas in the United Kingdom, where there is only one tier of government, the local District authorities are responsible for the urban highway system. Elsewhere responsibility is split between the county and district levels of government.

In metropolitan areas, other than London, public transport is controlled by Passenger Transport Authorities, which delegate responsibility for operations to independent Passenger Transport Executives. Rail-based services are mostly provided by the national railway company and in London by a regional authority. Urban bus services have been deregulated and are provided by a mixture of private and publicly-owned companies.

In Sweden, like many other countries, the municipalities have sole responsibility for water supply and sewerage and for streets and highways. In some areas, however, local

38

municipalities have joined forces to create special regional bodies for water supply and/or sewage treatment.

Municipalities are also responsible for bus and rapid transit services, while regional transport authorities are responsible for intra-regional rail services.

In Germany, there is a clear distinction between the traditional municipal responsibility for such things as roads and sewerage networks and the delegation of responsibility to separately-constituted municipal enterprises, which cover a variety of urban services, including water supply, heating, gas and electricity and public transport. The enterprise form is obligatory for water supply and for urban areas with more than 10 000 inhabitants. Nonetheless these enterprises are typically small, since their operations are confined to the municipality in question.

To overcome this problem of size, some municipal enterprises are joined together in different forms of voluntary association. The German experience is described in greater detail below (Inset 1).

In Australia responsibility for the major components of infrastructure in the larger urban areas usually rests with State government. Local councils' responsibilities are mainly confined to the local street system and surface water drainage, though some additionally have responsibility for water and sewerage. State government powers are often exercised through statutory public authorities, such as the Sydney Water Board.

In the United States, however, there is more devolution of responsibility. While State government retains a direct responsibility in most cases for the major highway and freeway networks, in many States, notably California, more reliance has been placed on single-purpose "governments" – i.e. directly elected bodies charged with providing and financing the provision of a single service, such as water supply or rapid transit. By contrast New York and Boston represent the polar opposite, where large multi-purpose city governments are responsible for providing the full range of infrastructure services.

2. The search for efficiency

Behind the concern with organisational and managerial structures there lies a deeper concern with the efficiency and responsiveness of urban infrastructure planning and provision. In a climate of fiscal restraint, there is an overriding need to ensure that urban infrastructure and its related services are provided in the most efficient manner possible.

A number of potential sources of inefficiency have been identified in the traditional public sector organisation and management of urban infrastructure.

Diseconomies of scale

It is debatable whether there exist positive economies to larger scale in the provision of urban infrastructure.

Small organisations enjoy advantages of flexibility and proximity to their clients. But they often pay a price in terms of the need for external co-ordination.

The most important sources of economy related to size are probably:

Inset 1. The municipal multi-purpose enterprise in Germany

The German experience is interesting because it is largely based on the notion of multi-purpose enterprises. This approach was frequently found in a variety of countries; but in many it has been abandoned.

German cities are responsible for the supply of electricity, gas district heating, water supply and public transport. If they decide to operate these works themselves, they have to create their own city works outside the normal municipal budget.

In the ideal case the city works (*Stadtwerke*) is the operator of all the services mentioned. However, this is true only in some larger cities: the average city works in smaller cities and towns provides only two or three services. A more recent development is the proposal to include also waste-water treatment and solid waste disposal.

The city works operate on a commercial basis, because they use commercial accounting systems and draw up balance sheets and profit and loss statements. Corporation tax has to be paid on profits made. Losses incurred, for example on public transport services, can be deducted. The works are run mostly in the special form of *Eigenbetrieb* which is strongly attached to the city administration. The alternative form is either a normal limited liability company (*GmbH*) or a joint stock company (*Aktiengesellschaft*) of which all the shares belong to the city.

The activities of the works are usually restricted to the city area; but sometimes surrounding areas are included. The largest of such enterprises, the *Stadtwerke München,* had a turnover of DM 2.5 billion and 10 000 employees in 1988. But the average city works are much smaller.

The multi-purpose concept (*Querverbund*) gives management the possibility to co-ordinate the work of different functions. The concept should be seen in contrast to other European countries where companies often provide only one service, but on a nationwide basis: e.g. gas and electricity services. It can achieve significant "synergistic" benefits. According to a recent survey by the *Stadtwerke Bochum,* the separation of responsibility for different services would in theory halve the profits made. The *Stadtwerke Düsseldorf* calculates that it saves nearly one quarter of the investment cost by laying gas and water pipes together. The co-generation of electricity and district heating, which is popular in many cities, can also save large amounts of energy.

For the city itself a better planning co-ordination of its activities is also possible. An example is the joint use of graphical information systems, often paid for by the *Stadtwerke.* Another example is the application of energy supply concepts which help to reduce atmospheric pollution and promote energy saving[18].

Possible diseconomies due to small size are thus compensated at least in part through the municipal enterprise form. Its limitations are reached, however, when infrastructure plants have to be built and operated which cannot be run economically at a local level – such as very large power plants.

- *Managerial and staffing economies.* Larger organisations can afford to employ managers and professional staff of a higher calibre than small authorities; the risk, however, is that larger organisations quickly become "top-heavy".
- *Financial economies.* In systems where there is a degree of financial devolution, larger organisations are usually able to obtain better terms from the capital market and are better equipped to manage their cash-flow and to obtain maximum returns from such things as the investment of liquid funds on the short-to-very-short term money market[19].

On the other hand, the value of technical economies of scale, where these exist, for example in the design and operation of waste-water treatment plants, has to be set against the very high cost – when real interest rates are high – of the "indivisibility" of the investment, if this implies investment in surplus capacity in advance of demand.

The differentiated nature of the possible economies suggests that careful attention needs to be given to the requisite organisational structure: simple size is not an adequate criterion.

Professionalisation

Responsibility for the planning and management of different types of urban infrastructure has in many cases become the preserve of particular professions. The introduction of efficiency criteria and economic or accountancy practices as major elements in the decision-taking process is often resisted on professional grounds. Well-established professional guidelines and rules-of-thumb may be threatened by the apparent invasion of new ideas and personnel. A particular facet of the clash between the economic approach to planning and programming and, for example, the engineers' approach, that is the cause of much disagreement in contemporary conditions, is the variability of the solutions proposed by economists as a result of the volatility of the cost of capital. There remains a great need for mutual education and confidence-building between the relevant professions.

Inappropriate division of responsibilities

Efficient outcomes are only likely to arise if they can be assessed within an appropriately integrated framework. The division of responsibility for capital works and programming, on the one hand, and maintenance and operations, on the other hand, – to take only one typical example – between different organisations or levels of government, accountable to different constituencies, can effectively prevent the development of appropriate expenditure and management policies[20].

Blurring the roles of client and provider

Many public sector bodies responsible for infrastructure, especially directly-elected bodies, attempt both to represent and articulate the views of the clients of infrastructure and to act as supplier. This confusion of roles, it has been alleged, leads inevitably to inefficiency.

The lack of competition

Most urban infrastructure services are usually regarded as natural monopolies. As such, it is accepted as inevitable that a single organisation will assume control of the provision of services and expenditure.

But this is not a legitimate inference. What matters is whether or not the monopoly is contestable.

In practice the barriers to competition in the provision of major infrastructure come often from the entrenched advantage which ownership of the existing network gives to the current provider and from the difficulty of establishing a "level playing field" between public and private organisations. Private organisations pay taxes, but also enjoy tax benefits, for which there may be no equivalent in the case of public sector organisations.

Public transport services are the one case where competition is feasible and where there is some chance of establishing neutrality between the conditions under which public and private bodies would compete.

Short of full privatisation, however, which does not necessarily increase the level of competition, there are numerous ways in which elements of the provision, maintenance and operation of urban public infrastructure services can be opened up from time to time to competition: for example, through a competitive search for ways of providing and financing the provision of new basic infrastructure[21]; through the competitive operation of services (e.g. public transport services); and through the competitive development of management systems.

Inappropriate incentives

Public infrastructure authorities tend to lack appropriate managerial and organisational incentives to develop efficient operational and investment policies. The multiple objectives established for public organisations tend to rule out the sort of simple, profit-oriented incentives which operate in the private sector. But the institution of performance measures, combined with more sophisticated requirements for monitoring and reporting on the conduct of their affairs, offers a partial alternative. But there remains a need for the development of stronger incentives.

Public sector organisations are often also reluctant to introduce incentives into their dealings with suppliers and clients.

In a simple example, the use of bonuses for the early completion of road construction contracts in the United Kingdom led to a 40 per cent reduction in time for no additional cost[22].

3. New approaches to management

In recent years there has been an increasing tendency to draw into the public management of infrastructure approaches and models that are well

Cost or profit centres

Each component of the organisation is established as a separate entity with its own budget and target outturns. Internal "cross-subsidies" are minimised and intra-organisation transactions are fully costed and accounted for.

While most public sector organisations have traditionally encouraged delegation of responsibility for current costs and technical matters to departmental managers, the full-scale devolution of responsibility goes much further. In particular it requires local or departmental managers to address three central concerns:
- *The cost of capital.* The costs of borrowing are fully allocated to separate activities and an appropriate return is expected on all capital employed.

- *Labour costs and industrial relations.* Individual managers are directly responsible for improving labour productivity and for related bargaining over wages or conditions of employment.
- *Revenues.* Wherever possible revenues are attributed to specific activities and budget outturns; in addition managers are encouraged to look for new sources of revenue and to take a much more positive stance in relation to marketing.

Return on capital

The performance of separate departments or activities is assessed directly in terms of its contribution to the overall return on capital employed.

Managerial performance

As a corollary, individual managers are given much greater responsibility, and freedom, to develop and implement strategies for their departments, subject to the overall targets and budgets established for the organisation as a whole.

In return for a substantially greater degree of accountability managers may also be eligible for direct financial rewards for successful outcomes.

The integration of these private sector approaches to management has not always proved to be easy. In particular there is a marked conflict between the private sector approach to management accountability and remuneration and the traditional public sector approach which tends to emphasize job security and formalised wage and salary scales.

However, the scope for increased efficiency is often substantial. For example, the establishment of cost centres and intra-organisation accounting allows departments to compare the costs of internal suppliers of intermediate services – such as maintenance or transport – with external private sector providers. Similarly the need to meet budgetary targets encourages managers to confront differences in labour practices and wage costs compared with external contracting.

4. Recent and innovative experience

The recent experience of some OECD countries points to a number of important and interesting ways of responding to these problems (Inset 2). The initiatives reviewed here all relate to developments wholly within the public sector. The involvement of private organisations and capital is reviewed later in Chapter 7.

In the United States many infrastructure services are supplied by "single-purpose" governments or special districts – i.e. elected authorities responsible for only a single service. While this creates greater incentives for specific efficiency in relation to the category of infrastructure in question than when it is managed by a multi-purpose government, it is still often the case that the resulting organisations are too small to be truly self-supporting[23].

In Germany the well-established model of the municipal enterprise, is in part an attempt to meet these objectives.

To get round the problems of small scale in Germany moreover larger regional entities have been formed, though these have been criticised for restricting the development of local, indigenous approaches – for example, to the solution of environmental problems. Large single-purpose organisations, for example for water supply and sewage treatment, have also been created in some areas – e.g. the Ruhr and Stuttgart. These are essentially the product of associations of municipalities. They do not have charging powers in their own right.

In the field of public transport, loose associations have been formed in a number of major metropolitan areas throughout Germany to co-ordinate the planning and operation of services. However, these *"Verkehrsverbund"* do not have the status of integrated enterprises.

Good information and a high level of skill on the part of managers are a part of the justification for the creation of larger-scale organisations in Germany. In Sweden by contrast, where the same problems are recognised, more reliance has been placed on the role of national associations. For example, the Swedish Association of Local Authorities and the Swedish Water and Waste Water Works Association play a significant role in the dissemination of "best practice" information and in the training of municipal personnel.

Advanced training of this type and the dissemination of information also help to break down any unproductive barriers that exist between different professional groups.

In Sweden, moreover, an attempt has been made to separate within some municipalities their role as client from their role as producer of infrastructure and services. The client unit is made responsible for determining what services should be provided and for specifying goals in terms of the level of service. The producer unit is responsible for providing the service and for productivity. This division of labour also opens the way to a degree of competition, since tenders can be called for the provision of a defined level of service.

The results of this experiment, however, are controversial. It provides no guarantee of greater overall efficiency and responsiveness, even if on occasions it has proved beneficial.

In the State of New South Wales, in Australia, plans to "corporatise" certain infrastructure authorities, including water and sewerage, rail and bus services are under discussion. The model for this is the programme of corporatisation undertaken by the New Zealand government in relation to nationally-owned business activities[24].

By corporatisation is intended a structure that resembles as closely as possible that of a private business but where the share-holding remains exclusively, or for the most part, public. This has many similarities with the German concept of municipal enterprise discussed above, though the intention is that each service should comprise a distinct organisation.

However, there are problems with achieving a satisfactory degree of correspondence to the private sector model for three main reasons:

- the differential tax treatment of public and private organisations: complete equivalence would entail a substantial transfer of resources to the another level of government – in this case the Federal government since it is the body responsible for taxing corporate income – away from the State;
- the lack of actual or potential competition, except in the case of bus services: this reflects the entrenched advantage of the current infrastructure providers; and
- the uncertainty that surrounds the removal of government under-writing of debt, since it is debatable whether government could in fact allow its creatures to default on its obligations.

The model depends heavily on the role of improved managerial incentives to efficiency and on the absence of political interference. It remains to be tested how strong these incentives would be in practice and to what extent politicians would respect, and the public would accept, the abrogation of their right to interfere in the conduct of publicly-owned undertakings.

In the United States, many States and local infrastructure authorities have developed methods of Capital Improvement Planning, designed to identify capital improvement priorities for a period of 5 to 6 years. The aim is to provide better information about the range of available options and their costs and benefits. Unfortunately the adoption of such methods has not been so successful in reducing the costs involved in the delay between planning and executing new programmes.

In addition to the need for improved data systems and maintenance programming, authorities in the United States have highlighted the need for improved techniques for the resolution and prevention of disputes – especially in the politically sensitive area of environmental protection – as critical to improving the efficiency of infrastructure management and reducing costs. The removal and updating of unnecessarily restrictive or inappropriate regulations have also been the focus of attention.

In Italy a recent law relating to the reform of local authorities has introduced legal autonomy for existing local government entities responsible for the provision of infrastructure. The aim is to assist the process of modernising management structures. In addition a system for evaluating the performance of local service suppliers is to be established.

Proposals for organising multi-sectoral urban holding companies in the larger Italian cities – similar to those already serving regional governments and to those in Germany, discussed above – are also under consideration. There is a strongly-held view that this type of structure is most likely in the Italian context best to meet the joint goals of management efficiency and political responsiveness.

Finally, in the United Kingdom, responsibility for public transport policy and finance in the major metropolitan areas (outside London) has been transferred from local councils to Passenger Transport Authorities. The aim of this shift of power was less to achieve economies of scale in the strict sense than to achieve the benefits of the better co-ordination and planning of services. Although the United Kingdom experience differs from that of Germany, in that in Germany the association is voluntary while in the United Kingdom it was imposed by the national government, there are obvious similarities in the underlying objectives.

The United Kingdom has also attempted to improve efficiency throughout the delivery of local public services by establishing an Audit Commission. This body is charged with improving management practice and finding ways of increasing efficiency in addition to the traditional function of auditing local government accounts[25]. Its role in disseminating ideas of "best practice" has helped both to improve efficiency at the local level and to draw the attention of central government to issues where new policies or initiatives would be advantageous.

5. Policy options

To improve the efficiency of urban infrastructure there is a need to tackle the main sources of inefficiency. The main lines of development should include the following:

Division of responsibilities
1. *There is a need to link closely investment decisions with maintenance responsibilities.* Capital works and programming, on the one hand, and maintenance and operations, on the other hand, need to be better integrated.
2. *The areas of political and professional responsibility should be demarcated clearly.* Undue interference between decision-makers and managers should be avoided; accountability of the providers of urban infrastructure should be improved and public participation in the design and operation of this infrastructure – especially when they have an impact on the environment – should be increased.

Improving the efficiency of public sector provision
3. *There is a need for performance targets, as well as for economic and financial targets.* Efficient anagement and effective use of available resources require that

managers should have clear goals. Performance targets should directly reflect the objectives of public policy. New measures of performance may need to be established, together with improved mechanisms for monitoring the achievement of objectives. Economic and financial targets should be specified in terms of rates of return on capital used and assets (at current replacement valuation) and in the form of dividends payable, where appropriate.

4. *There is a need to develop incentives within the public sector.* Public infrastructure authorities tend to lack appropriate incentives to develop efficient investment and operational policies. Improved accounting methods and regular assessment of performance should be introduced and financial incentives should be established for managers, staff and workers.

5. *There is a need to introduce more competition.* Most urban infrastructures are still regarded as natural monopolies and the scope for competition remains therefore too limited. Even if privatisation is not desired, there are numerous ways in which the provision, the maintenance and the daily operation of urban public infrastructure services can be opened up to competition.

6. *There is a need to better respond to user preferences.* Public authorities which are responsible for urban infrastructure provision should establish a close "dialogue" with the users of this infrastructure. The corollary of a more competitive public sector provision of urban infrastructure is that public authorities need to become more sensitive to market demand. This will require closer liaison with customers and appropriate surveys to enquire about changing needs.

7. *There is a need to better account for the environmental impact of urban infrastructure.* The design and management of urban infrastructure should be based on principles of environmental acceptability and sustainable development. The achievement of environmental objectives should become an integral part of infrastructure planning and operation (e.g. through environmental impact assessments). Existing urban infrastructure which is not environmentally satisfactory should be modified accordingly.

Chapter 6

PRICING AND FINANCING IN THE PUBLIC SECTOR

1. Underlying economic issues

The twin aims of improving the efficiency of urban infrastructure provision and facilitating its financing come together in the development of appropriate pricing policies.

Pricing policy is itself designed to enhance efficiency. At the same time the revenues generated provide the basis for financing investment, maintenance and renewal.

This section of the report is concerned only with developments within the public sector. Equivalent developments that involve or relate to private capital are discussed in the following section.

2. Pricing and charging policy

Pricing or charging policy can improve efficiency in two ways:
- by encouraging more efficient utilisation of existing infrastructure; and
- by providing improved signals about the potential value of new investment.

The role of infrastructure pricing is predominantly limited to rationing the privately-appropriable benefits that urban infrastructure creates for individuals and businesses. But at the same time, pricing can be used to impose on consumers the cost of negative external effects, such as pollution, caused by their consumption. However, it cannot cover all forms of external effects nor can it take into account the public goods characteristics of urban infrastructure (if indeed there are any).

The distinction between urban capital infrastructure and the current services associated with its use is significant in this context. An efficient pricing regime should be designed to cover (and hence to finance) both the cost of the capital involved and the current costs of the related services (for example, of operating urban rail services). However, for various reasons, including both the difficulty of financing capital investment by borrowing (discussed further below) and the availability of grants or subsidies from higher levels of government, the link between the financing, and hence the pricing, of the two components of infrastructure services (the capital and the current) is often in practice broken.

This is also true where regulations limit the ways in which the cost of capital can be reflected in the price charged to users. In Germany, for example, local entities are often only permitted to recoup historic costs. As a result pricing policy remains a problematic element in the development of effective economic policies for urban infrastructure. There is often a straightforward clash between the requirements of an efficient pricing system, which include that the cost of capital be incorporated in the overall marginal cost, and the existence of limitations on the long-term funding of debt.

As the recent OECD report on water supply[26] makes clear, the financial (and often institutional) distinction between capital charges and current costs masks a more relevant distinction between the incremental cost of additional infrastructure capacity and the cost of connection or access to the systems. It is the exclusion of the first from the short-run marginal cost perceived by consumers or users that can lead to excess demand. The separation between the financing of capital and current costs can also create difficulties in relation to the comparable treatment of "old" and "new" infrastructure.

3. Marginal versus average cost pricing

Economic analysis suggests that the appropriate basis for pricing policy should always be the marginal cost of infrastructure[27].

Two sources of concern which commonly lead governments to deviate from this principle – the distributional implications and the impact of inflation – are considered separately below.

In practice therefore the requirement that prices should be based on marginal costs – in relation to capital assets – is equivalent to the charging of their full replacement cost.

Unfortunately this too is an area where the implementation of sound economic principles is often upset not merely by direct political intervention but by statutory and legal restrictions or interpretations[28].

4. Investment analysis

More efficient pricing policy can also assist investment analysis.

Since urban infrastructure creates many "external costs and benefits", an overall cost-benefit analysis is essential if sound investment decisions are to be taken[29].

Cost-benefit analysis of this type is routinely required in relation to highway investment involving national funds, for example, in Germany and the United Kingdom.

This analysis needs to be undertaken with care, since much of the received wisdom about the effects of infrastructure is not confirmed by the evidence[30].

There is also a need for consistency of analysis between categories of infrastructure where user charges play a larger or smaller role in total financing. To accept or reject investment in one category of infrastructure on the basis of an overall cost-benefit analysis, while in the case of another the decision is based solely on a financial rate of return, is clearly misguided[31].

But efficient pricing helps to indicate more clearly the real extent of the benefits derived by users.

5. The role of grants from higher levels of government

One factor which has militated against the adoption of efficient pricing and investment practices for urban infrastructure in many countries has been the availability of grants from higher levels of government.

While it can of course be argued that the aim of a system of grants is to increase the supply of infrastructure beyond the level that local communities can afford, there is no doubt that the effect has been to distort the pattern of spending on infrastructure and to get in the way of charging users a price that genuinely reflects the long-run cost of the infrastructure[32].

6. Pricing and the optimisation of maintenance expenditures

A further aim of pricing policy should be to establish an appropriate balance of expenditures between new investment and asset maintenance or replacement. By sending the right signals about the strength of demand in different areas and for different types of infrastructure pricing policy can provide a critical input to management planning.

Overall expenditures on urban public infrastructure are often inefficiently distributed between new investment, replacement and maintenance. This may be due either to a failure to analyse correctly the appropriate balance of expenditure or to institutional or budgetary constraints such as the separation of responsibility for investment and maintenance or arbitrary constraints on capital or current spending. The effect of an inappropriate distribution is to reduce the overall return on the management and operation of infrastructure. Peterson, for example, reported a very wide variation between United States cities in the willingness to offset the real economic depreciation of the urban road system by appropriate maintenance outlays[33].

The failure to dedicate adequate expenditure to maintenance and replacement also reflects a more general ignorance about the true rate of capital consumption. General estimates of the overall condition of urban public infrastructure, as recommended in the United States, for example, by Hatry and Peterson[34] and in the United Kingdom by the Water Research Centre[35], can provide essential base data for the formulation of expenditure priorities. Analysis of the true rate of capital consumption, as in the exploratory studies undertaken in South Australia by Burns, can assist both in the forward planning of budgets and in the design of appropriate pricing and charging mechanisms[36].

The optimal distribution of expenditure between new investment and the maintenance and replacement of existing facilities depends critically on the real cost of capital. According to Lesse and Roy, when the cost is high, maintaining infrastructure in prime condition or neglecting maintenance until the infrastructure is sufficiently deteriorated to warrant full replacement may be the only sensible options: the assumptions built into their analysis indicate that other courses of action are sub-optimal[37]. Socially and politically, however, a solution that falls somewhere between the two is bound to be preferable. More careful economic analysis is required[38].

7. Management accounting as a basis for pricing policy

Closely related to the issue of pricing, and to the better management of maintenance and renewal expenditures, is the system of financial accounting employed by urban public authorities, since it is on the basis of costs, as accounted, that prices are set and policies are developed.

In many countries the traditions of public sector accounting remain different from those generally employed in the private sector. In the United States, for example, the antiquated approach to accounting is thought to be one of the main barriers to the adoption of an efficient pricing system in the water supply industry. Public sector accounts are typically based on cash-flow transactions, that is actual expenditures and receipts. Private sector accounting more commonly adopts an accrual basis.

The move to accrual accounting has been put forward as one way in which public authorities can achieve greater efficiency, through a more realistic assessment of the true value of their assets.

8. Pricing policy under conditions of constrained borrowing and high interest rates

Where access to borrowed funds is limited for reasons of macroeconomic policy and the cost of capital is high, efficient pricing policy has to be reconciled with minimal reliance on borrowing and with alternative sources of finance. (The scope for adjustment to high real and nominal interest rates is discussed briefly in Annex 1.) Direct limits on borrowing typically take the form of statutory or constitutional limitations on bond issues (as in the United States, for example) or formal or informal controls imposed by higher levels of government (as in the United Kingdom and Australia).

Indirect limits on borrowing follow from constraints on the volume, or the use, of revenues which reduce the amount of new debt-service that can be accommodated within the budgets of infrastructure authorities. There are many different types of example, from the constitutional limitations on local tax increases instituted in the United States to the controls on the rate of increase of public utility charges currently in force in Germany and Australia.

These limitations reflect the wide-spread view that reductions in public debt are necessary to create the conditions for stable, inflation-free economic growth, whether regionally or nationally.

The effect has been to encourage infrastructure providers away from the traditional reliance on *publicly-funded debt** to more innovative ways of financing urban infrastructure. There is a risk as a consequence of upsetting the aim of achieving greater efficiency through improved pricing policy.

In fact on many occasions there is a direct contradiction between the macroeconomic imperative which requires borrowing to be minimised and the objective of microeconomic

---

* *Publicly-funded debt:* Public sector longer-term borrowings secured against the "full faith and credit" of government or undertaken by an agency of government with at least an implicit government guarantee.

efficiency which would dictate that long-term investment in infrastructure should be funded and amortised over an equivalent period.

The dilemma has been well described by Terny and Prud'homme who pointed out that *"in the first place* ... it is hardly to be expected (let alone wished) that the growth of fiscal capacity will provide, in coming decades, a source of finance for public infrastructure ... [and]*in the second place,* recourse to borrowing does not seem able to take the place of taxes and to allow a growth in public expenditures."[39]

9. Distributional issues

Popular concern about pricing policy in relation to urban infrastructure and related services is usually focused on the distributional implications of a "user-pay" approach to financing.

Urban public infrastructure services (with some exceptions) tend to be "natural monopolies". This has been one of the continuing justifications for public involvement in the provision of infrastructure. But, as a number of writers have recently noted, another defining characteristic of public involvement in the provision of services is its concern with horizontal equity, equity between individuals[40].

There are three main categories of distributional effect associated with the provision of urban infrastructure: inter-personal; inter-areal; and inter-generational.

Issues of inter-personal equity are best treated outside the sphere of pricing policy. Modification of pricing structures to achieve distributional goals is rarely effective – in the sense of being well targeted to defined groups – and often carries a high cost in terms of general inefficiency.

Inter-areal equity is also better achieved through mechanisms other than pricing policy.

Inter-generational equity, on the other hand, is central to any efficient regime of prices. It is particularly critical where investment in infrastructure is subject to large-scale indivisibility. This can be the source of substantial inequity if the cost of infrastructure designed to meet future demands or needs is imposed on current users. What is needed is some means of financing the costs of infrastructure during the period before it is required.

A brief discussion of these distributional issues and possible approaches to them is contained in Annex 2.

10. Pricing policy in relation to specific categories of infrastructure

Streets and highways

There is a long-standing difference of view in relation to highways between those who regard the effect of the combination of vehicle taxes/fees and taxes on such items as petrol or diesel fuel and tyres as a form of "pricing" of highway use and those who regard these imposts purely as excise taxes. While vehicle fees and other such taxes can certainly be regarded as elements of a cost recovery system for inter-urban highways, there is more general agreement that there exists nothing equivalent to a full marginal cost pricing system for urban roads where the external costs of congestion assume much greater importance[41].

The efficiency of a system of road tolls also depends on the costs (direct and indirect) of collecting the toll. The potential costs of disruption or delay are much higher in relation to urban traffic than on inter-urban highways.

In the absence of a full system of urban road pricing (or area licensing), such as has been developed in Singapore, there are few opportunities for direct charging for the use of urban highways. These include bridges, tunnels and similar facilities and limited-access tollways. In general, the pricing of a few parts of the urban road system, the major part remaining unpriced, is not conducive to improving the overall efficiency with which the system is used. While it is true that time-savings are typically a much more important determinant of usage than money costs, the imposition of substantial tolls on parts of an urban network is bound to distort the distribution of traffic on the system as a whole. The collection of tolls moreover itself creates additional delays.

Water and sewerage

There is much more opportunity to ration the use of water, and access to the sewerage system, by means of consumption-related charges. A recent OECD report[42] has reviewed in detail the arguments for pricing and the experience of different countries. It concludes that charges related to consumption, for example the so-called "increasing-block" tariff widely used in Japan, can contribute significantly to encouraging more efficient utilisation of water resources and of the infrastructure associated with water and sewage disposal without losing sight of equity objectives. New technological advances are permitting the introduction of, for example, seasonal and peak-period differentials.

In practice local public authorities responsible for waste water treatment are sometimes reluctant to charge the full cost to users on the grounds that "downstream" consumers also benefit from clean water[43]. However, this is fundamentally inconsistent with the "polluter-pays" principle.

Surface water drainage

Infrastructure designed to control and channel surface water run-off provides a good example of a case where the benefits are clearly appropriated by individual property-owners but formal pricing (in the form of a current charge related to the benefit enjoyed in any given period) is not practicable.

In Germany, flood protection and surface water drainage are treated as "public goods" to be financed out of general revenues; but storm sewers are financed from user charges and cities make a direct contribution out of tax revenues to cover the costs of surface water run-off.

Public transport

Efficient pricing of urban public transport has tended to be limited by two factors:

- the technical problems involved in introducing differential charges for peak and off-peak services; and
- the economic concern with diverting passengers from using cars onto public transport.

The latter argument, which has been given renewed force by the recent experience in some countries of the effects of increasing public transport fares, notably in London, reflects a broader concern with the efficient utilisation of the urban transport system as a whole. Less-than-marginal-cost pricing is justified by the absence of equivalent means of ensuring efficient rationing of the use of the highway system.

11. Recent experience with direct user charges

There is a wide-spread recognition of the importance of pricing policy and of its potential contribution to the financing of infrastructure.

Water and sewerage

The area where innovation is most obvious is in relation to water and sewerage. Most countries, which have recently been reviewed by OECD, report a high percentage of costs covered by some type of "user charge"[44].

In Japan, such charges are widely used: about 60 per cent of the cost of waste-water treatment and disposal are recouped from user charges.

In the United Kingdom, by contrast, there is virtually no use of water metering and up to now payments have been related to the local tax base and not to the use of water.

In France user charges are the predominant, and in most cases the only, source of revenue for water and sewerage.

In Sweden the median percentage of costs covered by fees in 1987 was 76 per cent. However, there was a wide spread between areas, with some covering 100 per cent of costs from user charges while others covered under 5 per cent.

Recourse to increased user charges to finance extensions of the water and sewerage systems in Spain, notably in Madrid, however, has met with considerable political opposition.

In Canada, about 84 per cent of water supply costs and 56 per cent of sewage collection and treatment costs are recouped from user charges.

Four types of rates are used in Canada for the pricing of water supply: flat rates, declining block rates, increasing block rates and constant rates. A survey of 470 municipalities by Environment Canada in 1987 indicated that 37 per cent of the population was subject to flat rates, 34 per cent to declining block rates and only 2 per cent to increasing block rates. Twenty-seven per cent faced a fixed charge for each unit of water consumed.

By contrast increasing block tariffs are particularly common in Japan, where according to the OECD report cited above 52 per cent of water authorities are using them.

The attraction of increasing block tariffs is their distributional implications: large-scale users tend also to be the richer households.

It is estimated that in Finland between 70 and 80 per cent of the cost of water and sewerage is recouped from users.

In Germany by contrast local authorities are required to recover the full cost of waste water collection and disposal from users (although a 15 per cent allowance from taxes is permitted to cover the cost of handling the run-off from streets).

However, since in many areas German local authorities are only permitted to depreciate historic costs, the requirement for a full "user-pay" system, even including a return on capital, does not meet the conditions necessary for an efficient pricing system. Still less does it provide a revenue base for further capital investment.

This type of legal limitation is in many countries a barrier to the achievement of an efficient pricing regime.

Other barriers come from controls on the rate of increase of prices – often fixed at or below the current rate of general price inflation – and from the prevalence of grants or subsidies from higher levels of government.

In the United States, as a report prepared for the National Council on Public Works Improvement noted in 1987, "the historically low level of water rates has been perpetuated by the 'fiscal illusion' that water supply is inexpensive. [There is] also a belief – associated with the service view of public water supply – that, as a basic necessity, water should be inexpensive"[45]. While there is a wide-spread shift towards full-cost pricing, local resistance to increased government charged and antiquated accounting procedures are contributing to delay the process.

The Italian government since 1987 has promoted new laws designed to bring the rates charged for local infrastructure services more closely into line with costs. In the case of water the permitted basis approximates 100 per cent cost recovery. However, there remain significant regional differences in the implementation of pricing policies. In Northern Italy, where autonomous enterprises are the norm, there has been a general improvement in the rate of cost recovery. However, in Southern Italy the results have been less satisfactory.

Roads and highways

There have been no serious attempts yet in developed countries to follow the example of Singapore in introducing forms of direct "road pricing" (except in Oslo and Bergen, Norway). Apart from taxes on vehicles and fuel, the only price mechanism is exercised through parking control.

The topic is often discussed; and there have been a number of active proposals. Recent examples include the attempt to exclude "non-essential" traffic from the centre of Rome and a proposal for a system of licences to control the entry of vehicles into the centre of Stockholm.

The rate of technological advance gives some grounds for believing that road pricing is closer to becoming a reality.

However, there are many examples of tolls being charged for specific crossings, such as bridges or tunnels, within urban areas. For example, a law of 1986 in France authorised communities to charge tolls for specific facilities of this nature in urban areas for the first time. The power is limited, however, to projects whose cost is greater than a minimum threshold (FF 100 million at 1986 prices) and permits only the recoupment of actual expenses (including loan charges, amortisation and maintenance).

The ear-marking of vehicle registration fees and taxes on fuel and other automotive products as proxies for direct charging is more common. In the United States, for example, it is estimated that more than two-thirds of all Federal expenditures – mainly in the form of grants to State and local governments – are now directly derived from user charges. A recent report in Australia has recommended a uniform national system of road user charges, with statutory definition of the "general taxation" and "user charge" components of revenues derived from motor vehicle users.

This form of cost recovery, however, represents at best only a form of "average cost" pricing. It can make only a limited contribution to the costs of urban roads and highways, which are typically much more expensive than inter-urban facilities, owing both to the high opportunity cost of land and to the prevalence of congestion. In urban areas efficient pricing of road space is more difficult to achieve.

Public transport

In almost all countries public transport fares, for services operated by public enterprises or organisations, are set below their full cost level. In Germany, for example, only 62 per cent of public transport costs were covered by direct receipts in 1986. In Canada the equivalent figure was 50 per cent. In the United States, according to a report prepared for the National Council on Public Works Improvement, the figure in 1984 was as low as 29 per cent[46]. In Sweden only about 42 per cent of the cost of regional and local rail services was recouped from fares in 1987; in Stockholm the nominal loss was SKr 2.8 billion and fares covered only 34 per cent of costs.

In France a major part of the cost of public transport is paid by employers through the *Versement Transport*. This is a form of payroll tax (limited to incomes up to the social security contribution ceiling), which is currently set at up to 2.2 per cent in Paris and 1.5-1.75 per cent in provincial cities. However, the combined income from the *Versement Transport* and direct user charges is still not sufficient to cover the full cost of public transport services.

In Japan by contrast many urban rail services are privately-owned and are regarded as profitable.

The main justification for setting fares below full cost is the need to attract commuters away from private car use. Environmental arguments are also now used to justify this approach.

However, there is increasing recognition of the fact that, while these may constitute good grounds for subsidy, the low percentage of revenue derived from public transport users often also masks wide-spread inefficiency. Costs are high; labour productivity is low: utilisation of capital equipment is poor.

Some countries supplement direct subsidies for urban public transport by indirect subsidies. For example, in France employers are required to reimburse one half of the cost of their employees' weekly or monthly public transport passes, while in Japan there is no limit on the amount of employees' fares in the large metropolitan areas that employers may reimburse. In both cases the cost is tax deductible for employers and tax-exempt for employees. By contrast, in many countries such as Australia and the United Kingdom, any contribution by employers to their employees' cost of travel to work is taxable in the hands of the employee.

12. Experience with alternatives to direct user charges

Alternative arrangements fall into two categories: those that are limited to improving efficiency and those that at the same time attempt to overcome the underlying financing constraints.

One alternative to direct user charges is ear-marked taxes. If these taxes relate to costs imposed or benefits received they have some of the efficiency characteristics of user charges. However, they do not absolve the public authorities from the responsibility for raising capital.

Ear-marked taxes

Ear-marked taxes have often been criticised, especially by economists, on grounds of the inflexibility that they introduce into the allocation of resources[47].

The potential advantage of ear-marked taxes arises, however, from the effect of limiting public infrastructure authorities' sources of finance and revenue to this source. Unable to increase revenue in any other way infrastructure providers are induced to look for ways of becoming more efficient. In return for a degree of inflexibility, there is scope for considerable efficiency gain.

Ear-marked taxes exist in a number of countries.

In France the *Taxe Locale d'Equipement,* the *Versement Transport* and the *Taxe sur les Espaces Verts* are all examples of ear-marked taxes whose revenues are dedicated to aspects of urban infrastructure and planning. The first is mainly applied to infrastructure works[48].

In Japan equivalently the City Planning Tax and the Business Establishments Tax are both designed to assist with the financing of urban infrastructure.

In the United States such taxes have a very long history, dating back to the origins of the Special Assessment system in the 1920s. The more frequent form of the tax in the period from 1945 until recently was the Special District system. This combined the ear-marking of taxes with the establishment of single-purpose governments with responsibility for particular services or categories of infrastructure.

This system was undoubtedly the main instrument for facilitating new urban development, and the required provision of infrastructure and services, in large parts of the United States – notably California – during the major building booms of the immediate post-war period.

More recently there has been a return to the Special Assessment model; but the more important development of *capital fees** is described in more detail in the section that follows.

---

* *Capital fees:* Fees or charges imposed on land or property, whether or not in process of development or redevelopment, on a "once-for-all" basis (often as a result quite large – in money terms) used to defray the costs of capital works. (As opposed to *recurrent charges,* which may similarly be used to finance capital works but go to meet debt-service payments.)

An assessment of the impact of ear-marked taxes in the United States in the period following the so-called tax-payers' revolt of the late-1970s suggests that, in the context of otherwise highly constrained revenue sources, they can contribute to encouraging efficiency gains in the provision of infrastructure services.

An alternative form of the ear-marking of taxes for infrastructure in the United States followed the near-collapse of the local fiscal system in cities like Cleveland, Ohio. There, in return for agreement to increase local income tax, one-half of the increase was ear-marked for infrastructure improvement[49].

In New South Wales, Australia, the State government has recently imposed an increase in the State tax on petroleum products, the proceeds of which have been ear-marked for upgrading the highway system.

Financial devices

Other alternatives to direct user charges can be divided into those that attempt to close the gap between financing costs and actual or potential revenues; and those that rely on capital contributions as a substitute for current revenues dedicated to debt-service and operating costs.

Both these approaches reflect the two dominant concerns of governments, with restrictions on their borrowing capacity and with the impact of high real and nominal interest rates which generate cash-flow deficits in the early years after investment.

Two methods of closing the gap between financing costs and revenues are by means of:

Indexed finance

Experience in this regard seems to have been limited, most indexed financing schemes having been restricted to the financing of rental housing, as in Denmark.

Governments have shown reluctance to expand the use of this type of financing instrument to other categories of investment. This reflects also the limited acceptance of indexed finance by the capital markets.

A recent example is the financing of a tunnel under Sydney Harbour for which a major portion of the capital was raised through index-linked bonds.

Leasing and related mechanisms

Leasing is well established in a number of countries, including the United States, Germany, Canada and Australia as an alternative to the debt-financing of selected components of infrastructure[50].

However, in most cases the financial effectiveness of leasing depends on the appropriation by the lessors of tax benefits which they would not otherwise have been able to obtain. This approach was often of particular value to financial institutions which otherwise lack significant tax offsets.

Property Funds or Trusts, as in Germany, and sale-and-leaseback, as in the United Sates, are other ways of reducing the effective cost of capital through the accrual of tax allowances or deductions.

In many countries, however, reliance on these approaches for financing public infrastructure has been short-lived and they are now effectively banned by the relevant tax authorities. This is because the effect of leasing and similar initiatives is to transfer the burden of meeting finance costs from the budgeted sources of revenue to the general taxpayer. In relation to public infrastructure this is seen to be unacceptable, though the practice remains available to the private sector.

Capital contributions

Yet another approach has been to try to substitute capital payments or contributions for current revenue streams, in order to reduce the public sector's need to finance infrastructure through borrowing.

Such contributions can be made consistent with the objectives of an efficient pricing policy, provided that the basis for levying capital charges is the benefit (or potential benefit) that will be derived from the provision or replacement of infrastructure.

Indeed capital contributions may be more effective that direct "pricing" in some cases – e.g. financing highway extensions and improvements – exactly because the imposition of current user charges is impractical or undesirable.

Capital contributions also have the great merit that they can be levied on potential (or future) beneficiaries, as well on the property of the initial cohorts of users of particular components of the infrastructure. In this way they can contribute to overcoming some of the problems associated with the "indivisibility" of many categories of infrastructure.

However, to maintain a local fiscal system that is both efficient and equitable in the way in which tax burdens are distributed may require consequential adjustments to the incidence of general taxes. A number of studies have expressed concern about the potential for inter-personal and inter-generational inequity if this issue is not addressed[51].

Developer contributions and exactions

Examples of up-front capital payments as contributions to the cost of urban infrastructure exist in most countries. The extent of reliance on this form of financing, however, varies significantly.

Up-front contributions may take the form of financial payments or of provision of infrastructure in kind. The latter is the form often preferred by land developers.

Contributions are usually mandated in accordance with prescribed schedules; but alternatively, or in addition, individual contributions may be negotiated with developers.

The system is most widely used in relation to new urban development which entails the conversion of land from non-urban to urban use. But it is also used in cases of redevelopment.

In the majority of countries developers are required to provide most of the immediately local infrastructure, including local streets, curbs and drainage, sewer and water reticulation and some open space, at their own expense.

The United States has extensive experience of this form of cost recovery. Exactions, as they are there known, to cover the cost of infrastructure have been widely used, especially in States like California and Florida, where the rate of new urbanisation remains high.

The development of this form of financing was given renewed emphasis after the so-called tax-payers' revolt of the late 1970s which dramatically restricted the ability of governments to raise revenues and to enter into general obligation debt.

Throughout the United States the use of exactions to finance infrastructure is hedged around by strict legal requirements. These usually include:
- the establishment of a clear nexus between the works to be financed and the parcels of land on which the charges are to be levied;
- the strict ear-marking of funds; and
- fair apportionment of the burden of cost.

Despite these limitations, the courts in many parts of the United States have been favourably disposed to the initiation of systems of exactions by the public authorities. They have accepted that it is a natural extension of the State's "police power" in relation to new development and that without recourse to such financing instruments development would simply not be able to occur in a climate of local fiscal restraint.

One significant implication of the requirement for "fair apportionment" of the burden of cost is that charges are often levied on existing land-users as well as on the developers of new urban communities. Moreover, in many cases they extend to "future beneficiaries" – that is to say, the owners of parcels of land expected to be ripe for development in the foreseeable future but still in pre-urban use. To this extent the legal requirement is consistent with the economic principles of efficient and equitable pricing.

During the 1980s an attempt was made in many parts of the United States to move beyond the traditional form of exaction for infrastructure – clearly linked, through the nexus of benefit, to particular parcels of land – to a more general form of levy. This was based on a broader conception of needs and costs falling on the community as a consequence of new development (or more often redevelopment) – such as the need for more low-income housing or improved public transport. To distinguish them from exactions, these charges are often referred to as *linkage fees.**

Here the courts have been much less willing to accept the right of local communities to penalise particular developments or land-owners. Attempts to institute linkage fees have been overruled by the courts or by referendum in a number of communities and are statutorily outlawed in at least one State.

However, linkage fees have been accepted in some cities. For example, they have been instituted successfully in San Francisco and Boston to finance (through cash payments or works "*in lieu*") low-income housing and, also in the first case, improvements to public transport.

---

* *Linkage fees:*A special case of impact fees, whose proceeds are dedicated to purposes that have some "linkage" to the development but which cannot be said to be a direct or immediate requirement consequent on it: main examples – the need for more low-cost housing and public transport, "linked" to downtown office development.

An interesting variant on the exaction system has been adopted in Houston, Texas. This involves levying Capital Recovery Charges for waste-water treatment plants, similar to *impact fees.** But unlike fees, these charges guarantee those paying access to adequate capacity to meet their needs.

In many parts of the United States, such as Orlando, Florida, prospective connection charges are used as collateral for the raising of short-term capital to undertake infrastructure works.

Experience in other OECD countries

Connection charges for water and sewerage are found in many countries including Finland and Sweden. But they often cover only the costs of reticulation and some contribution to trunk mains. They exclude the cost of "headworks".

In Germany, capital contributions are levied on incoming residents and are limited to 90 per cent of the cost of works. But, as noted above in the case of the United States, existing land-users or owners are also liable for assessment.

In Japan, powers exist under the City Planning Act for the levying of capital contributions; but, since they are not compulsory, some municipalities have been reluctant to take advantage of them. These powers have recently been supplemented by the "Beneficiaries-Pay-In-Due-Proportion" system which allows costs to be recovered from development over much larger tracts of land.

In France, a recurrent tax whose revenues are dedicated to local infrastructure works – the so-called *Taxe Locale d'Equipement* – has been in place since 1967. This was later supplemented by the system of *Zones d'Aménagement Concerté* which provided a basis for agreement between the public authorities and developers about sharing the cost of infrastructure – once again in terms of cash payments or direct works – in large development schemes.

This system was criticised, however, for leading to the "sale" of increased densities in return for contributions to infrastructure costs and for under-estimating the actual impacts of new development.

The scope for capital cost recovery in France has recently been supplemented by the designation of *Périmètres de Participation* or special exaction zones. The aim of this move was to introduce more formality into the informal systems of negotiated contributions that had grown up since the 1970s.

In the United Kingdom, by contrast, exactions of land for public infrastructure projects by means of conditions attached to the grant of planning permissions have been outlawed by the courts. In the case of highways, however, the authorities have relied on voluntary agreements which in effect have amounted to a system of contributions.

As a consequence of the privatisation of the water and sewerage industry (described below), the United Kingdom has also recently instituted a formal system of contributions

---

* *Impact fees:* Fees or charges (usually in capital form) levied on sites undergoing development or redevelopment to meet the cost of "off-site" public capital works required as a consequence of the development (e.g. for roads, schools, open space, etc.) or to mitigate adverse impacts (e.g. environmental pollution).

for water and sewer connections. In place of up-front capital contributions, however, the new system will depend on current "deficiency" payments. These will require land-owners to make good for a period of 12 years the difference between the proceeds of the relevant current charge and a share of the annual borrowing costs for the associated infrastructure.

In Canada, there is wide-spread use of capital contributions to finance infrastructure and many cities base their financial strategy on the expected income from this source.

In Australia capital contributions are payable usually only in relation to water and sewerage and in New South Wales for some additional local needs. However, they have hitherto generally been set well below the full cost of the requisite infrastructure.

Land readjustment (or land pooling)

In Japan, costs are also recovered through the Land Readjustment process.

The Land Readjustment system is also used for this purpose in France. But the experience of both countries is similar: it is difficult to initiate co-operation between land-owners and the requirement that a defined majority agrees to participate in the scheme has limited its success.

However, the system has been applied with some success in Western Australia; and a similar system is now under review in New South Wales.

13. Policy options

The design and implementation of appropriate pricing and financing methods should aim to meet the following goals:

Financing
1. **Capital budgeting should be better adapted to the real cost of capital.** Where the real cost of capital is high, it is essential to economise on capital expenditures. This entails a continuing search for more efficient and less costly technical solutions and a better phasing of expenditures.
2. **At the same time there is a need to find a solution to the inflationary enhancement of nominal interest rates.** Three practical alternatives are:
   - *Inflation-indexed capital finance.* This is an efficient solution to inflation but it depends on the acceptability of indexed paper to the capital markets.
   - *Shifting the financing burden from current debt service to up-front capital contributions.* The great advantage of this approach is that it transfers to developers, land-owners or land-users the responsibility for recourse to the capital market.
   - *Equity financing.* This solution depends on, and constitutes a potential rationale for, greater private involvement in the financing of urban infrastructure.
3. **Wherever possible, urban infrastructure authorities should aim to derive a substantial part of their revenues from ear-marked streams (including benefit-related tax assessments) and their borrowings should be secured against future revenues.** Reliance on ear-marked revenues, as opposed to general taxation, will improve account-

ability and encourage efficiency. Securing borrowings against revenues will ensure that investment decisions are related to future needs.

4. *Accounting by infrastructure authorities should be based on replacement cost.* The accounting that underlies management decisions must be based on a full appreciation of the economic cost of the use of the resources involved, which can only be achieved through up-to-date replacement cost analysis. The cost of capital and the value of assets should automatically be adjusted for inflation.

Pricing

5. *Pricing of urban infrastructure should be designed to approximate to marginal cost pricing.* This approach achieves the greatest overall efficiency. It entails two requirements: the use of an up-to-date analysis of replacement costs, appropriately depreciated, and a variation for significant peak loads and capacity constraints.

6. *All beneficiaries of urban infrastructure should contribute to its financing. User charges, linked with polluter charges, should be favoured.* The design of charging systems based on user charges should aim at the same time to incorporate pollution-related pricing mechanisms. This is particularly relevant in the case of water and sewage, as well as in the case of urban highways.

7. *Alternatives to direct user charges are up-front capital contributions (or charges) and beneficiary taxes.* The great merit of these approaches is that they are consistent with the policy objective of relating benefit to marginal cost, while at the same time they provide an up-front flow of funds that can reduce the need for public-sector borrowing in favour of urban infrastructure.

8. *Charges or taxes on urban development (or land values) that are intended to represent the price charged for new urban infrastructure should be distinguished from other taxes that may be used for general urban development purposes.* The aims of efficiency and equity require that general revenue-raising systems should not be mixed with the specific attempt to price urban infrastructure provision and maintenance.

9. *The distributional effects of pricing urban infrastructure should be taken into account.* A reasonable compromise between efficiency and inter-personal equity could be achieved by the use of basic entitlements or increasing block tariffs. Problems of inter-areal equity and inter-generational equity need also to be considered: for instance, it would not be equitable to load exclusively onto existing users of urban infrastructure the costs of providing capacity for the future.

Chapter 7

THE INVOLVEMENT OF PRIVATE CAPITAL AND MANAGEMENT

1. Background

The aim of attempts to shift some of the burden of providing and managing infrastructure onto the private sector is two-fold:
- to relieve the pressure on constrained public budgets, and more specifically to reduce the need for public borrowing; and
- to bring to the supply of infrastructure and related services some of the greater efficiency which it is believed exists in the private sector.

A precise analysis of the relative efficiency of the two sectors is confounded by the lack of a "level playing field". For this reason the establishment of comparable conditions for the supply and operation of urban infrastructure in the two sectors has become a central concern of some governments.

2. The advantages of private management and finance

Increased efficiency is seen to be the main benefit that will flow from greater involvement of private capital and management, apart simply from relief for constrained public revenues and borrowing capacity. The higher level of efficiency in the private sector is assumed to follow from a number of critical conditions:
- *Clarity of objectives.* Private sector managers are better able to pursue efficiency because the dominant objectives of private business are more clearly articulated.
- *Management autonomy.* Private sector managers are given greater freedom and authority to achieve their aims without undue outside interference.
- *Continuous assessment of performance.* The capital markets provide continuous assessment of the performance of private business and establish goals for management to achieve.
- *Managerial incentives and rewards.* Private sector managers' rewards are tied more closely to their achievement of corporate objectives.
- *Access to equity participation.* Equity finance provides advantages and a discipline, that is not available to public enterprises.
- *A competitive environment.* Private business normally conducts its affairs within a competitive environment which provides an additional spur to efficiency.

3. The cost of capital

Tax treatment is one especially important source of difference between the two sectors. Public sector organisations and, in some countries, quasi-government bodies, benefit from tax exemptions (at least in relation to significant categories of tax, such as corporate income tax)[52]. Ironically, however, the consequential lack of tax shelter, for example, in relation to debt-servicing costs, has in recent years meant that public sector organisations face higher costs. They cannot take advantage of the "tax efficient" methods of financing available to private sector organisations, such as structured gearing and leasing.

It has been estimated that in the United States these tax advantages may account for up to one half of the apparently greater efficiency of private suppliers[53].

Another consideration is the higher cost of capital typically paid by private corporations than by the public sector. It would be wrong, however, to interpret this as implying that the real cost of private supply is always higher than the cost of supply in the public sector. Insofar as the difference arises because the real risks associated with infrastructure provision and operation are reflected in the cost of capital to a private organisation, while the borrowings of the public sector are in effect secured against its reliance on taxation to avoid any possibility of default, the higher cost is in fact a better reflection of the true cost of infrastructure supply.

The involvement of private capital has taken a number of different forms. Some, notably full privatisation, can be regarded as involving the full transfer of responsibility for infrastructure onto private organisations. Others are hybrids, involving some elements of privatisation, while retaining elements of more traditional public sector responsibility.

4. Forms of involvement

The most common forms include:
- specifically negotiated contributions;
- establishment of joint public-private organisations;
- formal joint venturing;
- contracting out;
- granting of concessions;
- privatisation.

Not all examples of the involvement of private sector interests in joint organisations or ventures, however, entail a transfer of functions from the public to the private sectors. Co-operation between the two sectors can also perform a more political role in establishing the need for infrastructure works and agreement about their financing. The political good-will of private interests may be as important to the success of programmes for infrastructure renewal or maintenance as direct financial involvement[54].

5. Procedural considerations

The involvement of private capital in providing and operating urban public infrastructure inevitably raises difficult issues in relation to maintaining the public interest. The pursuit of public objectives remains paramount; but it cannot always be reconciled with the objectives of private providers.

There is a clear need for procedures to ensure that public interest considerations are not swamped in the attempt to make involvement attractive to private interests.

Machinery for the on-going regulation of private infrastructure provision is also very likely to be needed; but this cannot be so onerous as to constitute a disincentive to private sector participation.

6. Recent and innovative experience

Specifically negotiated contributions

Specifically negotiated contributions to the cost of urban infrastructure entail only the provision of finance. Responsibility for management and investment remains with the traditional public authorities.

The distinction between a "negotiated" contribution and a required payment (or investment in kind) is necessarily a fine one: the more so, since successful negotiation by the public authorities usually depends on the public authorities' having a reserve armoury of powers of compulsion. As with the up-front fees or charges discussed above, an alternative to financial payments is provision in kind.

The main difference between specifically negotiated contributions and a more generally applied system, such as has been discussed in Chapter 6 above, is that the latter is based on a formula of general application, while the former reflects *ad hoc* considerations. It is thus reasonable to regard a generally applied regime as an exercise in public sector pricing policy, rather than as a method of attracting private capital.

Somewhere between these two approaches falls the system of "incentive zoning". In return for specific contributions of a "public interest" character developers are granted additional development rights. This system has been adopted by many States and cities in the United States. The "over-density" contributions (under the so-called *Plafond Légal de Densité*) in France, instituted in the 1970s, were similar in effect. But these are now optional and many cities no longer have recourse to the system.

The volume and extent of the contributions to infrastructure that can be extracted from private developers through negotiation is potentially large[55]. The system has been applied very widely in the United States. Its success has depended on its acceptability to developers. In this connection it is therefore interesting to note that a major American developer, writing in defence of this approach, has said: "Developer contributions are investments more than contributions. They will be made when both the economic and political climates are attractive for investment."[56]

A recent example of a negotiated contribution in the United Kingdom is the proposed contribution by a private developer to the cost of a major extension of the London Underground. This is intended to facilitate and increase the value of a major redevelopment of former docklands on the south bank of the River Thames. It is a one-off payment, negotiated by the central government. While in some sense it sets a precedent, there is no automatic mechanism for ensuring that equivalent contributions will be made in other schemes.

The system of bonuses in return for contributions to infrastructure has also been used in the United States to generate large-scale private funding of local facilities[57]. But it has come under attack for undermining the rationale for the control of development by planning.

Establishment of joint public-private organisations

Joint public-private organisations take a multitude of forms. It is characteristic of recent developments in OECD countries that many have been custom-designed to suit particular needs or circumstances. There are few general models.

However, most joint public-private organisations fall into one or other of two categories:

- organisations charged with responsibility for a particular component of the urban infrastructure, for example a part of the rapid transport network or a link in the highway system, such as a tunnel or bridge; and
- organisations with responsibility for the development of a particular parcel of land, in the course of which they assume responsibility for providing all, or part of, the requisite infrastructure.

The second model is often based on the fact that the land or site in question is publicly-owned.

At the same time joint organisations may take responsibility only for managing infrastructure, or for financing and strategic policy and planning, or both.

In France joint public-private organisations are particularly common. The *Société d'Economie Mixte* (SEM) has a history that goes back more than fourty years. Originally mainly concerned with housing development and redevelopment – and in that context with the provision of associated social infrastructure – SEMs have expanded their field of operations to cover other categories of infrastructure, mainly in transport[58].

Despite the mixed composition of their capital, SEMs in France were originally dominated by the public sector. The shareholding by organisations other than national and local public authorities was usually a minority: the required minimum was 20 per cent. They were also heavily dependent on specialised public lending agencies, such as the *Caisse des Dépôts et Consignations*. However, this is less and less true, with the effect that SEMs are now emerging as more genuine exemplars of joint public-private participation.

Examples of SEM provision of urban infrastructure in France include the public transport system in Orleans and the rapid transit system (metro) in Marseille.

The *Sociétés d'Economie Mixte* in France are generally subject to the same tax regime as a private company, except in the case of certain urban redevelopment schemes and the draining of swamps where tax concessions apply.

However, it remains true that in countries which operate strict centralised controls on public borrowing, such as the United Kingdom and Australia, joint organisations modelled on the *Société d'Economie Mixte* would probably be classified as public sector organisations. They would not therefore represent a mean of avoiding public sector borrowing controls.

Joint public-private organisations are also well established in Japan. Current government policy actively supports the development of new means of co-operation between the public and private sectors. With this in mind, the government is concentrating on two approaches: the easing of regulations; and the provision of incentives. Examples of the easing of regulations include financial deregulation and the lifting of restrictions on the participation of telecommunications enterprises in joint projects, as well as a reassessment of some building and planning controls. Incentives are to be provided through the establishment of favourable tax treatment – for example, in the case of comprehensive resort areas – and the provision of some subsidies or low-interest finance. At the same time opportunities for further involvement through joint organisations in the provision of public utilities is to be encouraged.

A recent example of a joint public-private organisation, of which more details are included in Inset 3, is the Trans-Tokyo Bay Highway.

In the United States a similar joint public-private organisation was proposed for financing, constructing and operating part of the circumferential highway around Denver, Colorado. The aim of the association was to make possible the bringing together of tax revenues (derived from incremental land values and benefit fees) and private funds.

Inset 3.   **Public-private co-operation in urban highway construction and financing in Japan**

The Trans-Tokyo Bay Highway is planned to link Kawasaki in Kanagawa Prefecture to Kisarazu in Chiba Prefecture across Tokyo Bay. It will have a total length of about 15 kilometres. It will form part of the extensive network of trunk roads extending across the Tokyo Metropolitan Area.

A company financed by funds from the private sector, local public entities and the Japan Highway Public Corporation is being set up to undertake the construction and management of the project.

The Japan Highway Public Corporation will assume ownership of the highway and will be responsible for co-ordination of the project.

The steps in the process are as follows:

The Japan Highway Public Corporation obtains planning permission for the project and is granted the right to levy a toll by the Ministry of Construction.

Upon obtaining planning permission, the Japan Highway Public Corporation enters into an agreement with the Joint Company for the construction and management of the Trans-Tokyo Bay Highway.

The Japan Highway Public Corporation finances the basic survey work and any necessary planning adjustments; it acquires the land.

The Joint Company, on the basis of this agreement, raises the capital to finance the necessary preparatory work and the construction of the highway.

On completion, the Joint Company hands over the highway to the Japan Highway Public Corporation.

In return, the Japan Highway Public Corporation will reimburse the Joint Company for its expenses by dedicating to it a portion of the toll revenue derived from the highway over an extended period.

On completion of construction, a new management agreement is entered into by the Japan Highway Public Corporation and the Joint Company, under which the company will jointly be responsible for the maintenance and operation of the highway.

In Italy a joint public-private enterprise is being established to reclaim the basin of the River Po. This will incorporate schemes for waste water management and water purification.

Joint ventures between public and private bodies

Joint ventures between the public and private sectors differ from joint organisations in the degree of exposure to risk carried by the public sector.

In most joint arrangements with the private sector for the provision or management of infrastructure public bodies are largely protected against the risks of default by their private partners. In the case of joint ventures by contrast public and private bodies enter into the business as equal (or equivalent) equity partners. Each stands to lose if the project is unsuccessful.

In many countries it is difficult for the public sector to participate in such ventures exactly because of the exposure to risk. Special legislation may be needed to enable joint-venturing to go ahead.

Certainly there are those who argue that exposure to risk in this way is inappropriate, the more so since the public sector is putting at risk tax-payers' funds.

Owing to the commercial nature of the relationship between the private and public bodies involved, it is usually very hard to obtain detailed information about such ventures: the private sector insists on strict confidentiality.

The exact arrangements, however, are likely to reflect the circumstances in question. Certainly there is no requirement for exact equality of treatment, just as there is not between private parties to a commercial agreement. The arrangements should reflect the relative contributions that each makes to the project, though, less skilled in such arrangements, the public sector often lacks the bargaining power to obtain the best possible deal.

Owing to the lack of revenue-generating opportunities, such ventures are unlikely to occur in relation to many types of infrastructure. The most common contexts are those involving the development of land, where the risks are matched by the potential for profits.

In previous decades, what the public sector had to offer was often access to funds on favourable terms. For example, there were many joint public-private ventures in relation to city centre redevelopment in the United Kingdom in the 1960s, one product of which was usually improved transport facilities. These included better street layout, additional parking space and public transport interchanges. In return the public sector was able to finance a substantial component of the joint scheme.

Schemes that reflect this approach are still to be found in Japan, where public funds are available for joint ventures.

However, under today's conditions, where shortage of funds is one of the main motives driving the public sector to look for ways of involving the private sector, in many other countries this is no longer possible.

The main contributions that the public sector can make are: land; and development permission. These usually form the basis of the public sector's "equity" investment in joint ventures.

Thus in a major recent development in Los Angeles the public sector contribution was limited to a ninety-nine-year ground lease and development permission, in return for which it was expected to receive 15 per cent of the Net Cash Flow after eight years. There have been many similar examples in the United States in the course of the 1980s.

Such joint involvement in development schemes raises difficult issues also about the appropriateness of local public bodies' participating in development as principals. Many have been criticised for compromising their role as arbiters of development consent and as guardians of the public interest in the face of developers' proposals.

A recent joint venture on the outskirts of Adelaide in South Australia has involved a State government instrumentality providing land and guaranteeing the provision of some elements of infrastructure in return for a private developer financing and guaranteeing to undertake the provision of the remainder and of the housing, including housing for public allocation.

Other contractual arrangements

Short of full privatisation, there are many other types of contractual arrangement which the public sector can devise in order to involve private capital and management in the provision and financing of infrastructure.

The best known are contracting out (or "farming out") and the granting of concessions or franchises. These are discussed in more detail below.

The French experience, however, well illustrates the range and diversity of arrangements (Inset 4). They can be summarised as shown in table 4.

Contracting out

Contracting out specific services or elements of infrastructure provision and operation has become by far the most frequent way in which private skills and private finance have been drawn in.

It is very common for such things as construction and highway maintenance to be contracted out.

In Canada, some cities have decided to contract out their public transport systems. One study has found that this is more economical than direct provision[59]. Similarly, in the United Kingdom, following the general deregulation of urban bus services, local authorities are empowered to contract out, by means of tendering, subsidised services which they judge it important to maintain.

In France as much as 70 per cent of municipal water supply and treatment operations (outside the Paris basin) are contracted out to private companies. The municipalities retain ownership of the plant and determine strategic policy. They also regulate the prices that can be charged. They can dismiss the contracted company if they are dissatisfied with its performance.

In Germany the contracting out of the maintenance of sewers and water supply is widely practiced, especially in smaller towns and villages which lack the professional know-how for maintenance work.

In the United States the practice of contracting out local public services is now well-established. However, there are few examples in the field of infrastructure. This is partly because infrastructure provision and services too often have the characteristics of a "natural monopoly".

Concessions

The granting of a concession implies more than merely contracting with a private organisation for the management of infrastructure.

The granting of a concession is also sometimes referred to as franchising.

Concessions transfer to private organisations responsibility not merely for management but also for financing. In return the private organisation is usually granted greater freedom in the management and planning of the infrastructure.

The most frequent model of concession involves the public granting to a private organisation the right to construct, operate and manage infrastructure for a fixed time period after which the assets revert to the public sector: the so-called B-O-T, or Build-Operate-Transfer approach. Usually the time period is specified; but in some cases it is to be

Table 4. **Contractual arrangements between the public and private sectors in France**

Type of contract	Source of initial investiment funds	Management risk taking	Source of revenues
Concession	Private	Yes	User charges
Farming-out	Public	Yes	User charges
Management or direct administration	Public	No	Public funds
Works contract	Public	No	Public funds

left to be determined by the speed with which the private organisation is able to recoup the cost of its original investment, together with an appropriate return on the capital employed.

In many cases the granting of a concession itself involves the use of statutory or legislated powers which would not otherwise be available to a private body: for example, the right to expropriate land for the construction of rights of way. This is usually unavoidable in the case of major physical investments such as highways and rail transport.

Because most categories of infrastructure involve an element of monopoly, the private organisation is usually subject to some regulatory controls similar to those that might apply in the case of full privatisation. For example, in most cases the level and rate of increase of charges remains subject to control.

This involves a degree of risk to private capital. In return private organisations are increasingly inclined to demand that a part of the project risk be borne by the public authorities, for example in the form of a guarantee of revenues or asset values. The assessment of risk and its sharing between the parties to a concession agreement is a critical part of the process which demands careful attention by the public authorities.

Two forms of concession can be distinguished:

– those involving new facilities; and
– those that relate to existing facilities.

The first tend to be the more common, since the control that new investment implies is generally more attractive to the private sector. The public sector is also more likely to be seeking private capital to assume the burden of new investment.

One of the advantages of the concession system is that, like full privatisation, it can be extended to cover projects identified by the private interests themselves. This is consistent with the view that private entrepreneurs are often better than the public sector at identifying new investment opportunities. A good example is where the public sector holds land that is under-developed.

However, this is raising some new problems for the public authorities because of the potential for dispute over "intellectual property".

On grounds of efficiency and fairness, it is usual for the public authorities to use competitive tendering to ensure that concessions are granted to the lowest cost and most efficient providers. However, where private interests have identified a viable project that would depend on the granting of a public concession, they tend to believe that they have a proprietary interest in the proposed scheme. The issue of intellectual property is particularly difficult where governments invite proposals from private interests to take over, or supplement, existing public methods of infrastructure supply. Competitive tendering and the bringing-forward of new proposals are not easy to reconcile.

In Italy and France the construction and financing of inter-urban highways has been practiced for many years; but there are few examples in the field of urban infrastructure.

In Germany, concessions have been granted by municipalities, mainly for the construction and operation of sewage treatment plants. The practice is referred to as the "Operator Model". One such example is described in more detail in Inset 5.

In France, similarly there has been experiment with both the contracting out and with the granting of concessions in relation to local water and sewerage works.

The largest scale concessions for water and sewerage have been those granted for the northern and southern halves of the Paris basin. One of these is described in more detail in Inset 6.

In Canada, some municipalities have been reluctant to grant concessions in relation to public transport services, in part because they might then lose the benefit of subsidies from the provincial tier of government. Instead they have relied on contracting out the operation of the services.

There is extensive experience, in Japan, of co-operation between the public and private sectors in large-scale development projects and in housing and urban redevelopment. Moreover, some services, such as urban commuter railways, are wholly private. Nonetheless there appears to have been little experiment yet with the granting of concessions for urban infrastructure.

Inset 5. **Development of the private operator model for waste-water treatment in the State of Niedersachsen, Germany**

In 1984 the municipality of Wedemark in the State of Niedersachsen, Germany decided to improve its waste-water treatment. A technical and financial assessment was carried out. It was calculated that charges would have to rise by more than 35 per cent and that the municipality would have to borrow about DM 11 million to finance a new treatment plant. After a two-stage process the municipality awarded a contract to a private firm to integrate a number of smaller systems into a single larger and more modern system. It was estimated that the final cost would be about DM 20 million; but user charges were increased by only 5 per cent. In addition the municipality was able to sell its existing plant to the private operator for DM 3.6 million.

The plant will revert to public ownership after twenty-five to thirty years. In the meantime, the municipality is responsible for levying user charges. There is no direct contractual relationship between users and the private firm.

This model has been copied by a number of municipalities in the State of Niedersachsen. On average these have shown a saving of 24.5 per cent over the original calculation of the cost if the work had been undertaken in the traditional way by the public sector.

The cost savings are in part due to the adoption by private operators of more efficient planning methods, from which public operators could usefully learn.

In that the cost advantages of the private operator follow in part also from favourable tax treatment the true economic benefits of adopting the private operator model may be exaggerated.

Nonetheless the experience in Niedersachsen of the private operator model is attracting considerable attention from other parts of Germany.

In Australia, private consortia have undertaken the financing and construction of a major bridge in Brisbane and of the new Sydney Harbour Tunnel. The costs will be funded out of toll revenues. In the case of the Sydney Harbour Tunnel, the financing was based on the placement of inflation-indexed bonds issued by a major financial institution and on an interest-free loan to the private consortium, derived from existing Harbour Bridge tolls, during the period of the construction of the tunnel (Inset 7).

Tenders have recently been called in Sydney for the construction and operation of urban tollways, which will be integral parts of the city's grade-separated highway network, and the State government has awarded the first contract to a consortium formed by construction and consulting engineering interests.

In Italy, an association of private enterprises is to be licensed by the Veneto Region to finance and operate a system of acqueducts. The majority of the investment is to be provided by the private sector in return for a guaranteed minimum demand for water from the local distribution authorities and management control, while the lesser share of the investment will be provided by the regional administration in return for the right to control the tariffs (Inset 8).

Private financing of urban infrastructure in New South Wales, Australia

In New South Wales, Australia, the State government has made a major commitment to involving private capital in the provision of new urban infrastructure.

A tunnel under Sydney Harbour is being constructed and will be operated by a joint Australian-Japanese consortium. Short-run financing is in part from the proceeds of tolls on the existing Harbour Bridge which are being advanced to the consortium by the State government as an interest-free loan. The bulk of the capital cost is being funded through long-term inflation-indexed bonds placed by a major financial institution.

The operation of the tunnel and debt service will be funded out of the joint toll revenues of the tunnel and bridge. The consortium has the right to operate the tunnel for a period of thirty years after which it will revert to full public ownership.

The State government has invited tenders to provide grade-separated highway links within the Sydney metropolitan area. These also are to be financed out of toll revenues. One contract has been finalised. As in the case of the Harbour Tunnel, the highway will revert to public ownership and control after the agreed period. The State government will retain control over the level of the toll. However, the financing is being classified as wholly private, since the franchisee has to absorb all the risk associated with traffic volumes.

In the North-West sector of the Sydney metropolitan area, the statutory Water Board has signed a contract with a consortium of land-owners and land-developers. The consortium is financing and constructing water and sewerage treatment plant and distribution – in addition to the reticulation works normally carried out by developers on their own account.

In addition the consortium is putting up capital funds to have major road links necessary to the success of the development brought forward in the State's highway programme.

Capital finance for the project has been arranged through a major merchant banking institution.

The consortium directly owns only 36 per cent of the developable land in the area but it has assumed full responsibility for the initial infrastructure.

The public sector Water Board retains supervisory authority over the water and sewer system and will be responsible for operations. It will resume financial responsibility for the scheme three years after development commences. At this time it will take over the whole system for 64 per cent of its accrued cost, net of the contribution revenues that non-members of the consortium have paid who have commenced development before this date.

In this way the public sector is relieved of all the up-front cost of providing water and sewage treatment works and pipework and some of the cost of upgrading the highway network. It is also relieved of a substantial share of the risk for all time (relating to the parcels of land owned by the consortium).

However, since the consortium only in effect bears the risk in relation to its own land holdings, the residual portion of the cost has been defined as public borrowing (or more precisely as a financing arrangement) which counts against the State's entitlement to raise loans under the nationally-agreed system of public borrowing restrictions.

Privatisation

Experience of the full privatisation of urban public infrastructure is limited to a few countries. The principles, however, are clear[60].

Among the benefits of privatisation – and to some degree also of concessions – two in particular are receiving increasing attention:

– *The transfer of risk to the private sector.* Private capital is thought to be better attuned to estimating and accommodating risk and more efficient at minimising it

than the public sector. The public sector has not always been successful at estimating future demand or at controlling costs. Privatisation is intended to ensure that the failure rate is reduced and that the costs of failure are borne by the private capital.
– *Improved detection of investment opportunities.* The private sector is also thought better able to identify new investment possibilities, because of its entrepreneurial tradition. While the public sector often discusses a large number of theoretical possibilities, private capital, it is believed, will act more quickly to put into effect those that are viable.

On the other hand, it has been recently argued that the need to remunerate owners and managers (through fees and dividends) and the liability to taxes implies higher underlying costs for the private sector of infrastructure[61].

In theory full privatisation removes control over every aspect of the provision and operation of infrastructure from the sphere of public control (beyond those controls that normally regulate private enterprises). In practice, two categories of service have emerged:

– those totally free from controls; and
– those subject to regulation.

Public transport, specifically urban bus services, is the only current example where it has been thought reasonable to remove all specific regulatory controls. In the majority of cases, however, either because private infrastructure providers enjoy residual access to powers of compulsion – for example in relation to access to property or its acquisition – or because they enjoy an effective, and often incontestable, monopoly (or both), regulation is appropriate.

A significant corollary of privatisation for the public authorities, therefore, is the need to establish appropriate regulatory mechanisms. In countries where to date there has been little or no experience of the regulation of private utilities, this itself can prove difficult: the regulatory body is likely to need a "learning period" before it has sufficient experience, standing and precedent to perform its role effectively.

The lengthy and complex regulations that have been promulgated in the United Kingdom as a consequence of the privatisation of water services in England and Wales illustrate some of the problems involved[62].

Privately-owned water companies are well-established in the United States. They are subject to local price regulation. One analysis in the early 1980s showed that due to their easier recourse to the capital market they were much more likely to finance expansion out of revenue (retained earnings) and borrowings rather than out of up-front contributions or connection charges[63].

The United Kingdom has recently gone furthest in privatising urban public infrastructure.

In 1985 urban bus services were deregulated. The effect of this was to open the way for the establishment of wholly private services in all urban areas, though it did not of itself change the ownership of existing publicly-owned operations. In the event, however, several formerly public municipal companies have subsequently been privatised, as has the nationally-owned long-distance bus company[64].

The most recent example of privatisation in the United Kingdom has involved the establishment of ten water and sewerage companies, covering the greater part of England and Wales. Shares in these companies were subsequently offered to the public and the industry is now fully privatised. The success of the flotation undoubtedly depended in part on the valuable assets – mainly land – owned by the companies.

At the same time the United Kingdom government has established a new regulatory body. The functions of this body are described in more detail in Inset 9.

The United Kingdom government has also invited the private sector to make proposals for new privately-financed highways. These would be financed by tolls. A private company is currently constructing a new bridge over the Thames, which will be an integral link in London's outer circumferential motorway system.

Similarly two bridges in Dublin, Ireland, have recently been financed and constructed privately, to be funded out of toll revenues.

7. Overview of private involvement

The various ways in which private capital and management skills can be drawn into the provision and management of urban infrastructure need to be compared carefully in the light of the specific circumstances of each project or category of infrastructure.

The main differences arise in relation to:

– capital finance;

In September 1989 the United Kingdom government merged the existing authorities responsible for water and sewerage in England and Wales into ten new companies.

In December 1989 shares in these companies were offered to the public and allotted response to demand.

Existing customers and employees were given the opportunity to acquire shares on favourable terms.

The Water Act of 1989 sets out the framework for privatisation:

- the new companies are able to concentrate on water supply and sewage disposal and to diversify into other activities;
- capital funds do not come within government borrowing limits and will be raised on the private capital market;
- there will be better incentives to economy and the financial markets will play an important role in monitoring their success; and
- there will be opportunities for the companies to compete in the provision of commercial services in the United Kingdom and abroad.

At the same time the United Kingdom government has established a new regulatory authority, the Office of Water Services. This body is charged with:

- monitoring the performance of the new water and sewerage companies;
- overseeing compliance with conditions attached to their appointment;
- protecting the interests of consumers by limiting increases in charges and comparing the performance of companies to encourage efficiency; and
- ensuring that the companies' charges are fair.

- management control;
- strategic planning control;
- the exposure of the public sector risk;
- the need for regulation;
- the incentives to efficiency; and
- the effect on competition.

The characteristics of the different examples considered above can be summarised as in Table 5.

This matrix highlights some of the main differences between the examples discussed above.

There is no one approach which is clearly superior to the others. Each has advantages and disadvantages that suit particular circumstances or cases better or worse. It is very unlikely that one approach will be right in all circumstances.

Contemporary economic conditions inevitably point to the need to transfer some of the burden of financing urban infrastructure onto the private sector, just as they indicate a need for the public sector to learn from the private sector how to improve its efficiency. But this requires careful analysis of the specific characteristics of the situation facing the authorities responsible for urban infrastructure and the choice of an approach to involving private capital and skills that is appropriate to the specific case.

Table 5. **A comparative framework for evaluating alternative ways of involving private capital**

	A	B	C	D	E	F
Advantage to Public Sector						
Capital funding off-budget	Part	Part	Part/Full	None	Full	Full
Management control	Full	Part	Part	None	None	None
Strategic control	Full	Full/Part	Part	Full	None	None
Risk to public sector	None	Part	Part	None	None/Some	None
Need for regulation	None	None	None	Direct super-vision	Yes	Yes
Efficiency incentives	No	Some	Yes	Yes	Yes	Yes
Improved competition	No	No	No	Yes	Lmtd	Lmtd

Where: A = specifically negotiated contributions.
B = establishment of joint public-private organisations.
C = formal joint venturing.
D = contracting out.
E = granting of concessions.
F = privatisation.

8. Policy options

Policy aimed at drawing private capital and private management into the management and financing of urban public infrastructure should be based on the following:

General principles and forms of involvement

1. **The main objectives of involving private capital and management should be clearly established.**   In the field of finance, the advantages of involving the private sector are the transfer of risk, substitutes for public borrowing and up-front costs, and the protection of present users and tax-payers from the burden of paying for future needs. In the field of management, the private sector has often more expertise than the public sector, more specific technical skills, more sophisticated budgeting and accounting techniques.

2. **There may be a need to design regulatory mechanisms prior to the involvement of the private sector.**   The success of involving the private sector, the efficiency and equity of the result, will depend as much on the design of the regulatory framework as on the use of private capital itself.

3. **The form of private sector involvement should be selected according to specific objectives and local conditions.**   Involving the private sector in the financing and management of urban infrastructure can take alternative forms:

   – specifically negotiated contributions;

- joint public-private organisations;
- formal joint venturing;
- contracting out;
- granting of concessions;
- privatisation.

There is no single way of involving private capital and management expertise that is preferable in all circumstances. The choice of one of these forms of involvement will depend on local conditions and on the type of infrastructure considered.

Risks and prospects

4. ***The capacity of the capital market to absorb the additional demand linked to the provision of a new urban infrastructure, and the risks entailed, need to be taken into account.*** The successful involvement of private capital requires that the existing capacity and expertise of the private sector should be able to take on tasks which have generally been within the public sector. And in smaller economies such new tasks may entail capital inflow with undesirable consequences for the long-term balance of payments or level of foreign debt.

5. ***The risks for the public sector of involving private capital and management should be assessed.*** The corollary of transferring to the private sector the risks involved in investment in infrastructure is that they may prove too great for private capital to sustain, if economic conditions become adverse. The public sector must ensure that there are contingency plans and it must assess the likely extent of its own exposure.

6. ***In case of joint public-private ventures, the true value of the public sector's initial equity must be assessed.*** This may take the form of land or development rights or existing infrastructure, as well as the capture of existing revenues. Fair apportionment of the benefits of joint ventures depends on the design of schemes that are proof against changing economic conditions and that correctly reflect each party's initial investment.

NOTES AND REFERENCES

1. For a recent discussion of the relationship between urban growth and environmental concerns, see OECD (1990), *Urban Environmental Policies for the 1990s,* Paris.

2. For overall assessments of the state of urban infrastructure, see *inter alia*: U.S. National Council on Public Works Improvement (1988), *Fragile Foundations: A Report on America's Public Works,* Washington D.C.; National Economic Development Office (1986), *The Nation's Infrastructure,* HMSO, London; Economic Planning Advisory Council (1988), *Economic Infrastructure in Australia,* EPAC (Council Paper No. 33), Canberra; Broadbent, A. and Reidenbach, M. (1987), *Urban Infrastructure in Britain and Germany,* Anglo-German Foundation for the Study of Industrial Society, London; Martinand C. (1986), *Le génie urbain: rapport au Ministre de l'équipement, du logement, de l'aménagement du territoire et des transports,* La Documentation Francaise, Paris; Federation of Canadian Municipalities (1985), *Municipal Infrastructure in Canada: Physical Condition and Funding Adequacy,* FCM, Ottawa.

3. Argy, F. (1988), "Infrastructure and the Economy", *Dollars and Directions* (Proceedings of the Second National Infrastructure Conference), National Infrastructure Committee, Highett, Vic.

4. UK Standing Advisory Committee on Trunk Road Assessment (1986), *Urban Road Appraisal,* HMSO, London; in addition, European Conference of Ministers of Transport (1989), *Environment and Transport Infrastructure,* Paris, contains detailed examples of methods of reconciling the need for environmental, social and economic impact analysis.

5. Baumol, W., Panzar, J. and Wiling, R. (1982), *Contestable Markets and the Theory of Industry Structure,* Harcourt Brace Jovanovich, New York.

6. Aschauer, D. (1987), "Is the Public Capital Stock Too Low?", *Chicago Fed Letter,* No. 2, Federal Reserve Bank of Chicago, Chicago IL.

7. Sonnen, C. and Haney, M. (1985), *The Macroeconomic Impact of Accelerated Spending on Municipal Infrastructure,* Federation of Canadian Municipalities (updated 1988), Ottawa.

8. For a discussion of the underlying issues, see Burns, P. (1988), "Infrastructure Priority Setting" in *Dollars and Directions: Building Australia's Future,* National Infrastructure Committee, Highett, Vic.

9. Diamond, D. and Spence, N. (1989), *Infrastructure and Industrial Costs in British Industry,* HMSO for Department of Trade and Industry, London.

10. E.g. Nevile, J. (1987), "The Macroeconomic Effects of Public Investment", Appendix 5 to *Constructing and Restructuring Australia's Public Infrastructure* (House of Representatives Standing Committee on Transport, Communications and Infrastructure Report), AGPS, Canberra.

11. Mera, K. (1973), "Regional Production Functions and Social Overhead Capital: An Analysis of the Japanese Case", *Regional and Urban Economics,* Vol. 3, No. 2, pp. 157-186; and Mera, K. (1975), *Income Distribution and Regional Development,* University of Tokyo Press, Tokyo.

12. Hulten, C. and Schwab, R. (1984), "Regional Productivity Growth in U.S. Manufacturing, 1951-1978", *American Economic Review,* Vol. 74, No. 1, pp. 152-162.

13. Aschauer, D., *op. cit.*

14. Eberts, R. (1985), *The Role of Public Investment in Regional Economic Development*, Federal Reserve Bank of Cleveland, Cleveland.

15. Eberts, R. (1986), *Estimating the Contribution of Urban Public Infrastructure to Regional Growth*, Federal Reserve Bank of Cleveland, Cleveland.

16. Grieco, M. (1988), *The Impact of Transport Investment upon the Inner City*, Transport Studies Unit, University of Oxford, Oxford. Quotation from p. 15.

17. Hall, P. and Hass-Klau, C. (1986), "Can Rail Save the City?", *Revue U.I.T.P.*, Vol. 35, No. 3.

18. OECD (1987), *Managing and Financing Urban Services*, Paris, p. 82.

19. Also, the example of "revenue centres" cited in *Managing and Financing Urban Services, op. cit.*, p. 64.

20. Gakenheimer, R. (1989), "Infrastructure Shortfall - The Institutional Problems", *American Planning Association Journal*, Vol. 55, No. 1, pp. 14-23.

21. E.g. Stevens, B. (1984), *Comparative Study of Municipal Service Delivery*, Ecodata, New York; Smith, R. (1984), *Troubled Waters: Financing Water in the West*, U.S. Council of State Planning Agencies, Washington D.C., who cites examples of reductions in the cost of capital from improved competitive bidding.

22. Fawcett, M., "Britain: Renewal and Maintenance Strategies for Roads" *in* Broadbent, A. and Reidenbach, M., *op. cit.*, pp. 91-97.

23. Discussion in U.S. National Council on Public Works Improvement, *op. cit.*, pp. 64-65.

24. Boston, J. (1987), "Transforming New Zealand's Public Sector: Labour's Quest for Improved Efficiency and Accountability", *Public Administration*, Vol. 65, pp. 423-442, winter.

25. Davies, H. (1989), "External Audit of Local Government in Great Britain: A Corner of the Thatcher Revolution" in *Local Public Services and Crisis of the Welfare State* (Proceedings of an International Seminar organised by the Italian Ministry of the Interior), Rimini, Maggioli.

26. OECD (1987), *Pricing of Water Services*, Paris.

27. For a full discussion in relation to water and sewerage, see *Pricing of Water Services, op. cit.*

28. Discussion of average and marginal cost pricing in Canadian cities in Amborski, D. (1987), "Financing Infrastructure for Residential Growth in Canada: The Province of Ontario Case", *Planner (NSW)*, pp. 34-38, March.

29. Knox, P. (1988), "Public-private Co-operation", *Cities*, pp. 340-346, November.

30. U.S. Congressional Budget Office (1983), *Public Works Infrastructure: Policy Considerations for the 1980s*, Washington D.C.; p. 48 discusses some effects of public transport.

31. OECD (1987), *Toll Financing and Private Sector Involvement in Road Infrastructure Development*, Paris, pp. 42-43; also, Broadbent, A. and Reidenbach, M., *op. cit.*, p. 168.

32. E.g. U.S. National Council on Public Works Improvement (1987), *The Nation's Public Works: Executive Summaries of Nine Studies*, Washington D.C.; also, U.S. Congressional Budget Office, *op. cit.*, p. 61.

33. Peterson, G. (1986), "Urban Road Reinvestment: The Effects of External Aid", *American Economic Review*, Vol. 76, No. 2, pp. 159-164.

34. Hatry, H. and Peterson, G. (1984), *Guides to Managing Urban Capital*, The Urban Institute, Washington D.C.

35. National Economic Development Office, *op. cit.*

36. Burns, P. (1987), "Asset Replacement - Coming, Ready or Not", *Infact* (National Infrastructure Newsletter), August.

37. Lesse, P. and Roy, J. (1987), "Optimal Replacement and Maintenance of Urban Infrastructure", *Environment and Planning A,* Vol. 19, No. 8, pp. 1115-1121; Herz, R. (1988), "Urban Infrastructure Renewal", *Paper* to 16th PTRC Annual Seminar on Urban Management, University of Bath.

38. Hatry, H. and Peterson, G., *op. cit.*

39. Terny, G. and Prud'homme, R. (1986), *Le Financement des Equipements Publics de Demain,* Economica, Paris, p. 30.

40. Shoup, C. (1988), "Distribution of Benefits from Government Services: Horizontal Equity", *Public Finance,* Vol. 43, No. 1, pp. 1-18; Rothenberg, J., "Collective Versus Private Responsibility in the Financing of Public Infrastructure" *in* Terny and Prud'homme, *op. cit.,* pp. 317-340.

41. *Toll Financing and Private Sector Involvement in Road Infrastructure Development, op. cit.,* pp. 40-42, discusses the requirements for tolls to be effective; also, Goodwin, P. and Jones, P. (1989), *Systems of Infrastructure Cost Coverage (Road Pricing, Principle and Applications),* European Conference of Ministers of Transport (Economic Research Centre), mimeo, Paris; Ogden, K. (1988), "Road Cost Recovery in Australia", *Transport Reviews,* Vol. 8, No. 2, pp. 101-123.

42. *Pricing of Water Services, op. cit.*

43. U.S. Congressional Budget Office, *op. cit.,* p. 61.

44. *Pricing of Water Services, op. cit.*

45. *The Nation's Public Works: A Report on Water Supply* (1987), Wade Miller Associates Inc., p. 94, May.

46. Kirby, R. and Reno, A. (1987), *The Nation's Public Works: A Report on Mass Transit,* The Urban Institute, Washington D.C., p. iii, May.

47. U.S. National Council on Public Works Improvement, *op. cit.,* p. 59; Prud'homme, R. (1979), "Les fonctions de la fiscalité dans la planification des villes", *Proceedings 35th Congress,* International Institute of Public Finance; Stegman, M. (1986), "Development Fees for Infrastructure", *Urban Land,* pp. 2-5, May.

48. For a critical review of the *Versement Transport,* see Darbera, R. (1990), *Pourquoi il faut aussi penser du mal du Versement Transport,* Laboratoire d'Observation de l'Economie et des Institutions Locales, Paris.

49. Peterson, G. *et al.* (1984), *Guide to Financing the Capital Budget and Maintenance Plan,* The Urban Institute, Washington D.C., p. 9.

50. Discussion in relation to France by Chanet, J. *in* Terny, G. and Prud'homme, R., *op. cit.*

51. Stegman, M., *op. cit.*

52. Knox, P., *op. cit.,* p. 344.

53. *Toll Financing and Private Sector Involvement in Road Infrastructure Development, op. cit.,* p. 38.

54. The experiences of Cleveland, Ohio and Pittsburgh, Pennsylvania cited in Peterson, G. *et al., op. cit.,* p. 35.

55. *Toll Financing and Private Sector Involvement in Road Infrastructure Development, op. cit.,* p. 22, cites the example of a developer in San Diego, California, who was providing, financing, 33 separate infrastructure investments in connection with a major new land development; also, Jensen, H. (1988), "Developer Contributions", *Urban Land,* March; Cervero, R. (1986), "Unlocking Suburban Gridlock", *Jnl Am Planning Ass,* pp. 389-406, autumn.

56. Jensen, H., *op. cit.,* p. 37.

57. In the case of one major development in central Seattle, for example, it has been calculated that 28 of the resulting 55 stories were "earned" through 10 different contributions to "public interest" works; Lassar, T.J. (1990), "Great Expectations: The Limits of Incentive Zoning", *Urban Land,* pp. 12-15, May.

58. *Quarante Ans de Sociétés d'Economie Mixte en France* (1988), Economica, Paris; also, discussion in *Managing and Financing Urban Services, op. cit.,* p. 49.

59. Kitchen, H. (1986), *Local Government Enterprise in Canada* (Discussion Paper No. 300), Economic Council of Canada.

60. For a discussion of the theory and practice of privatisation, see Beesley, M. and Littlechild, S. (1983), "Privatisation: Principles, Problems and Priorities", *Lloyds Bank Review,* Vol. 149, pp. 1-20; Vickers, J. and Yarrow, G. (1988), *Privatisation: An Economic Analysis,* MIT Press, Cambridge, Mass.; Hemming, R. and Mansour, A. (1988), *Privatisation and Public Enterprises* (Occasional Paper No. 56), International Monetary Fund, Washington D.C.

61. Herrington, P. (1988), "The Economics of Private Water", *Economics,* pp. 106-110, autumn.

62. Available from the United Kingdom Office of Water Services, Birmingham.

63. U.S. Congressional Budget Office, *op. cit.,* p. 130; also, Yarrow, G. (1986), "Privatisation in Theory and Practice", *Economic Policy,* Vol. 2, pp. 324-377.

64. For a detailed evaluation of the United Kingdom experience of urban bus service deregulation, see Gomez-Ibanez, J. and Meyer, J. (1989), *Deregulating and Privatising Urban Bus Services: Lessons from Britain,* U.S. Department of Transportation (Urban Mass Transportation Administration), Washington D.C., January.

RESPONSES TO THE HIGH COST OF CAPITAL

The real cost of capital

High nominal interest rates entail a substantial burden of debt service. In the case of infrastructure, interest charges are absorbing an increasing share of available revenues. In many countries this is putting a great strain on the budgets of the organisations responsible for urban infrastructure.

It is not possible strictly to say whether high nominal interest rates are the product of an increase in the real cost of capital or merely imply the expectation of continued, and in some cases increased, monetary inflation. In relation to the current experience of inflation, however, the cost of capital is much higher in real terms than it was in the 1950s and 1960s; and this remains true even in countries where the public sector borrowing requirement has been significantly reduced. The implied scarcity of capital is particularly serious in relation to the supply of long-term capital-intensive facilities such as infrastructure.

The effect of high real and nominal interest rates is to break the link between the financing of infrastructure and its pricing. Where the true cost of infrastructure is given by an appropriate risk-adjusted real return on its current replacement cost, assuming amortisation over the period of its useful life, the initial cost of borrowing is likely to be considerably in excess of this. Cash-flow deficits are inevitable in the early years after investment.

The effects of inflation

The incorporation of anticipated inflation into nominal interest rates has the effect of concentrating the real burden of debt service into the early years of the loan period. This has two undesirable consequences:

- it introduces an inter-generational inequity into the distribution of the financing burden; and
- it reduces the amount of real capital formation that can be undertaken for any given level of potential revenue (or other source of current finance, e.g. inter-governmental grant) without incurring a nominal "loss".

Private sector organisations are to some degree protected against cash-flow deficits through the right to tax-offsets. Indeed many have turned this facility to their advantage. Public sector organisations, however, cannot equivalently transfer the burden to others without drawing on general revenues.

Inflation also increases uncertainty about the capacity of organisations to amortise debt and about the real level of financing costs. Only after the event is it possible to say accurately what the true burden of cost has been and how it has been distributed.

Possible adjustments

To mitigate the adverse effects of inflation the following solutions are available:

Pooling of historic and new debt

Since inflation also has the effect of depreciating the real burden of historic debt service, the burden of newly-incurred debt service can be lightened if old and new debts are pooled and "average" charges or taxes levied.

This is a practical method of dealing with the problem that is widely employed by public authorities. Its disadvantages are: that its efficacy depends on the historic mix of old and new debt – a matter of chance quite unrelated either to efficiency or to equity; and that it cuts across the notion of distributing an appropriate real burden, reflecting marginal cost, on those who benefit from each successive tranche of infrastructure investment.

Whether or not this form of cost pooling constitutes a "cross-subsidy", in the true sense, depends on how the resulting charges to the users of "old" and "new" infrastructure relate to an appropriate real rate of return on the value of the assets in question.

Capitalisation of the excess burden of debt service in the early years after investment

While some infrastructure authorities may be able to follow this course, at least to a limited extent, the capital markets generally look askance at the wide-spread capitalisation of cash-flow deficits by fixed-interest borrowers.

Inflation-indexed capital finance

This is an ideal solution from the perspective of public authorities but is rarely available in OECD Member countries. Both the capital markets and governments have been reluctant to adopt this approach to "monetary correction", mindful in part of the difficulties faced by those countries where the practice is now general. Indexed bonds, however, have been used successfully in some countries, for example in relation to the finance of housing in Denmark and Australia.

Equity financing

This is only available in the private sector and is one of the motives behind moves for increased private sector involvement in the financing of urban infrastructure.

The role of cross-subsidy

In practice, public infrastructure authorities often rely on much more widely distributed cross-subsidies to meet short or long-term financial deficits. For example, in Germany municipal infrastructure authorities have for years relied on profitable public services to subsidise the less profitable, though this practice is increasingly under attack. The practice of financing capital works out of revenue is also widely adopted as a partial solution to the problem; but the inter-generational implications of this are clearly adverse.

Annex 2

PRICING POLICY, FINANCE AND DISTRIBUTIONAL EQUITY

There are three main categories of distributional effect associated with the provision of urban infrastructure: inter-personal; inter-areal; and inter-generational.

These are considered in turn below.

Inter-personal equity

In the case of "priced" services (such as water or sewerage), where access to infrastructure services is traditionally financed (at least in part) by a system of specific taxes or charges, lower-income households or individuals pay a higher proportion of their disposable income for these services than those with higher incomes. At the same time, where charges are directly related to the level of consumption (as, for example, with metered water charges), lower-income households are likely to consume less.

This is of course no different from the situation that obtains in relation to the consumption of privately-provided goods and services. However, for services which are publicly provided and are regarded as basic or essential, this inequity is often regarded as unacceptable. A compromise between full marginal cost pricing and payment according to the means to pay (i.e. through taxes that relate to income or property values) has often been adopted: for example, a basic entitlement to the use of infrastructure services, financed by a tax that relates to ability-to-pay, with additional units of consumption chargeable at full marginal cost.

The OECD report on water pricing cites many different systems in relation to water supply, including some interesting examples from Japan of so-called increasing-block charges. In addition, some countries have experimented with rebates, or other reductions, for especially disadvantaged groups, such as the elderly, which take account of significantly below-average consumption needs.

The situation in relation to "unpriced" services (such as highways) is somewhat different. Individuals with different incomes make different calls on unpriced infrastructure services. Some services (e.g. highways) may have intrinsically greater use-value to higher income than to lower-income individuals. But there are no direct income-related barriers to the use of unpriced facilities.

Where charging and financing is based on up-front payments, as in the United States "special assessment" system, an additional consideration is the hardship caused to existing owners or residents by the requirement to contribute their share of the cost in a lump sum. Some groups – for example, those on low incomes or the elderly – may find it hard to obtain satisfactory credit terms to allow them to spread the cost over a period of time because of their intrinsically low credit-worthiness.

In this case an alternative, recently adopted in California, is to allow the liability for payment to be deferred until the affected property changes hands. This approach is common also in other countries. In Santa Monica, California by contrast up-front fees are paid by the municipality out of grants from higher levels of government in the case of households with an income less than 80 per cent of the median level.

Distributional issues are particularly relevant to investment criteria. Benefit measures based either on revenue generated or on direct assessment of value (e.g. valuation of time savings from transport infrastructure) both effectively weight the use of infrastructure by lower-income individuals by much less than its use by higher-income persons. As a consequence, there is likely to be a bias in the provision of infrastructure towards meeting the needs of the higher-income groups.

The use of average values is often proposed as one way of getting round this problem; but this may then be used to justify the provision of some services that turn out to be under-utilised, while for others there is excess demand. The essential need is for consistency of treatment between the criteria used for investment decisions (and related expenditure decisions) and the conditions actually affecting their likely future use. Unfortunately this is sometimes interpreted as being at variance with the pursuit of equitable or socially just practice.

Inter-areal equity

The demand for inter-areal equity usually arises because the provision and financing of urban infrastructure is organised on a territorial basis. Infrastructure authorities, or local jurisdictions with responsibilities for infrastructure, are established to serve the needs of businesses and residents within a particular geographical area. Local public finance systems in turn often involve the transfer of funds from higher levels of government, based, at least in part, on the principle of "equalising" fiscal burdens. The effect is to focus attention onto the differences between areas.

These differences may take the form of a different level of provision – one area may have a trunk sewerage system, another not; or one area may have access to a better highway network than another – or they may take the form of different taxes or charges or different taxing or charging systems.

In principle there should be no distinction at this level between an efficient and an equitable treatment of infrastructure. Equity is achieved, as is efficiency, when each area is fully provided with the level of services which can be justified by the excess of benefits over costs and when residents and businesses contribute to the real cost of infrastructure *pro rata* to the benefit they derive. Significant variations in either the level of service provided or its cost (or both) should be regarded as equitable, where, for example, they reflect significant differences in the real cost of provision. However, from the perspective of inter-areal equity, this is often unacceptable. There is often an explicit or implicit demand for inter-areal cost differences to be "averaged out".

Much of the concern with inter-areal inequities, however, stems from the failure of local infrastructure to meet the conditions noted above: e.g.

- where there is *under-provision* of services: on benefit-cost grounds provision would be justified, but, typically for budgetary reasons, investment in new infrastructure is delayed; or
- where *different charging systems* are in effect, so that the contributions paid by residents in different areas do not equivalently reflect the real cost of the infrastructure that has been provided; one common source of this type of divergence is historic cost pricing, which means that areas provided with infrastructure before others are likely to have lower charges.

Perversely a demand for inter-areal *inequity* has also at times been advanced as a means of improving the inter-personal distribution of access to infrastructure, where areas comprise relatively homogeneous populations of distinct social or economic standing. For example, it can be argued that the provision of public transport services should be more generous, or the level of water charges lower, in areas with a predominantly lower-income population. (This implies accepting a lower real rate of return on expenditures in some areas than others.) This example illustrates the great difficulty in reconciling the notions of inter-personal and inter-areal justice. Indeed, it is not uncommon for there to be a more radical conflict between them. For example, transfers designed to reduce charges or taxes in "high-cost" areas may well be used to reduce the payments made by higher-income residents, or by businesses, by more than those paid by lower-income residents.

In general, it is preferable for the goals of efficiency and inter-personal equity to take precedence over inter-areal equity; but political forces often dictate otherwise.

Inter-generational equity

Problems of inter-generational inequity arise acutely in relation to urban infrastructure because for the most part it has a long useful life. Two different issues need to be distinguished:

Distributing the cost over the life of the asset

To the extent that urban infrastructure is financed by means of current charges or taxes, the ideal must be that those charges/taxes should be distributed over the useful economic life of the asset. This often proves difficult for one or other of two reasons:

Amortisation of debt

It is almost impossible for public authorities to borrow funds for a term as long as the economic life of the infrastructure. As inflation has turned fixed-interest lending into a risky activity, so the maximum length of loans has been progressively reduced. Ten to fifteen years is commonly the longest period for public sector bond finance. Where public accounting practice permits once-only funding of capital investment, this can create severe inter-generational inequity: the burden of financing infrastructure is loaded onto the early years of its use; thereafter it is apparently "cost-less", a free resource.

(This remains true even where current taxes or charges are correctly adjusted to reflect a real return on the current replacement cost of infrastructure. In this case, unless the financing system allows for the capitalisation of unpaid debt charges, the short-term burden of financing investment in urban infrastructure, and the longer-run enjoyment of surplus, is transferred from the community of infrastructure users or beneficiaries to the wider community of taxpayers, whether local, provincial or national.) The refinancing of debt in order that the charges may be spread over a period more closely related to the economic life of the assets can contribute to improving inter-generational equity; but if interest-only terms are not available, the debt-service will still entail a premature amortisation component.

Inflationary enhancement of interest rates

Fixed-interest lending has to incorporate an inflationary component to compensate lenders for anticipated monetary depreciation.

The effect of this enhancement of the nominal cost of capital is to transfer the real burden of servicing debt to the early years of the repayment period (irrespective of the length of the amortisation). The effect is therefore similar to, but more acute than, the one noted above. Together they can have a marked impact on the inter-generational distribution of the cost of urban infrastructure.

Indivisibility and the burden of investment in advance of need

The second main source of inter-generational inequity stems from the intrinsic "lumpiness" of much urban infrastructure. This necessitates substantial expenditures in advance of need or use, the cost of which must be borne by the community in the short-run. When the real cost of capital is high, this entails a heavy burden, especially in areas of rapid urbanisation where substantial investment in anticipation of development is being undertaken. Where infrastructure investment is undertaken predominantly to improve the services available to existing residents, this problem is not so severe.

The first pre-requisite for allocating this burden is a thorough review of the engineering and other parameters which determine the scale of the infrastructure investment. It is often true that a succession of investments on a more limited scale is technically feasible and economically preferable. Unfortunately engineering and economic considerations are often seen to be in conflict: optimal investment programming is prevented by institutional or professional disagreement.

Some indivisibility is nevertheless inevitable. Those able to bear the short-run excess burden of cost include:

- *Current users of / beneficiaries from the new investment.* This is clearly inequitable, loading onto the "first-comers" a burden substantially in excess of their liability.
- *Current users of previously constructed facilities.* This rests on the historic depreciation of old debts discussed above. If the result is to improve the equity and efficiency of the charging system, it does so more by accident than by design.
- *Current tax-payers more generally.* This is the most commonly adopted approach. Excess debt service costs, in the short-run, are transferred to the wider community of tax-payers, whether national, provincial or local. The inter-generational effects are no better; but if the burden is small when widely distributed, considerations of inter-personal equity tend to predominate over inter-generational effects.
- *Willing lenders.* This is a sensible and equitable option. However, it depends on successful recourse to inflation-indexed loans, capitalisation of negative cash-flows and/or equity finance, as discussed above, if the burden of servicing debt is not to have the same adverse inter-generational effects.
- *Future beneficiaries.* The transfer of the excess current cost to the future beneficiaries or users of urban infrastructure is equitable, provided that they are capable of capitalising the cost.

The most common method adopted to effect a transfer of this sort is by means of a tax on those parcels of land which will benefit in future from the availability of infrastructure. This requires accurate assessment of the likely scope and rate of urban development if the imposition of charges or taxes is not to be unreasonably onerous. This in turn can act as a desirable brake on the design and implementation of infrastructure programmes.

The distribution of costs at the time of investment also acts as an incentive to the development of the parcels of land which the infrastructure is designed to serve. But it may prove onerous, and hence politically unacceptable, where the burden of advance cost is passed to small property-owners (or, in areas of existing development, to residents and businesses) who are not able to capitalise the burden without current hardship.

An alternative, recently adopted in California in connection with the financing of the new subway in Los Angeles, is to impose a tax on all the parcels of land expected to benefit from new infrastructure but to levy the tax only insofar as, and when, the value of the land actually appreciates. Snyder and Stegman have suggested that under conditions of inflation the carrying costs of facilities built to satisfy future needs will be onerous only where the initial expenditure is designed to accommodate a growth in demand greater than the rate of inflation[*]. Peiser has offered a formula for calculating an intergenerationally neutral schedule of charges for each successive cohort of infrastructure users[**].

---

[*] Snyder, T. and Stegman, M. (1986), *Paying for Growth: Using Development Fees to Finance Infrastructure,* The Urban Land Institute, Washington D.C.

[**] Peiser, R. (1988), "Calculating Equity-neutral Water and Sewer Impact Fees", *American Planning Association Journal,* pp. 38-48, winter.

WHERE TO OBTAIN OECD PUBLICATIONS – OÙ OBTENIR LES PUBLICATIONS DE L'OCDE

Argentina – Argentine
CARLOS HIRSCH S.R.L.
Galería Güemes, Florida 165, 4° Piso
1333 Buenos Aires   Tel. 30.7122, 331.1787 y 331.2391
Telegram: Hirsch-Baires
Telex: 21112 UAPE-AR. Ref. s/2901
Telefax:(1)331-1787

Australia – Australie
D.A. Book (Aust.) Pty. Ltd.
648 Whitehorse Road, P.O.B 163
Mitcham, Victoria 3132   Tel. (03)873.4411
Telefax: (03)873.5679

Austria – Autriche
OECD Publications and Information Centre
Schedestrasse 7
D-W 5300 Bonn 1 (Germany)   Tel. (49.228)21.60.45
Telefax: (49.228)26.11.04
Gerold & Co.
Graben 31
Wien I   Tel. (0222)533.50.14

Belgium – Belgique
Jean De Lannoy
Avenue du Roi 202
B-1060 Bruxelles   Tel. (02)538.51.69/538.08.41
Telex: 63220   Telefax: (02) 538.08.41

Canada
Renouf Publishing Company Ltd.
1294 Algoma Road
Ottawa, ON K1B 3W8   Tel. (613)741.4333
Telex: 053-4783   Telefax: (613)741.5439
Stores:
61 Sparks Street
Ottawa, ON K1P 5R1   Tel. (613)238.8985
211 Yonge Street
Toronto, ON M5B 1M4   Tel. (416)363.3171
Federal Publications
165 University Avenue
Toronto, ON M5H 3B8   Tel. (416)581.1552
Telefax: (416)581.1743
Les Publications Fédérales
1185 rue de l'Université
Montréal, PQ H3B 3A7   Tel.(514)954-1633
Les Éditions La Liberté Inc.
3020 Chemin Sainte-Foy
Sainte-Foy, PQ G1X 3V6   Tel. (418)658.3763
Telefax: (418)658.3763

Denmark – Danemark
Munksgaard Export and Subscription Service
35, Nørre Søgade, P.O. Box 2148
DK-1016 København K   Tel. (45 33)12.85.70
Telex: 19431 MUNKS DK   Telefax: (45 33)12.93.87

Finland – Finlande
Akateeminen Kirjakauppa
Keskuskatu 1, P.O. Box 128
00100 Helsinki   Tel. (358 0)12141
Telex: 125080   Telefax: (358 0)121.4441

France
OECD/OCDE
Mail Orders/Commandes par correspondance:
2, rue André-Pascal
75775 Paris Cédex 16   Tel. (33-1)45.24.82.00
Bookshop/Librairie:
33, rue Octave-Feuillet
75016 Paris   Tel. (33-1)45.24.81.67
     (33-1)45.24.81.81
Telex: 620 160 OCDE
Telefax: (33-1)45.24.85.00 (33-1)45.24.81.76
Librairie de l'Université
12a, rue Nazareth
13100 Aix-en-Provence   Tel. 42.26.18.08
Telefax : 42.26.63.26

Germany – Allemagne
OECD Publications and Information Centre
Schedestrasse 7
D-W 5300 Bonn 1   Tel. (0228)21.60.45
Telefax: (0228)26.11.04

Greece – Grèce
Librairie Kauffmann
28 rue du Stade
105 64 Athens   Tel. 322.21.60
Telex: 218187 LIKA Gr

Hong Kong
Swindon Book Co. Ltd.
13 - 15 Lock Road
Kowloon, Hong Kong   Tel. 366.80.31
Telex: 50 441 SWIN HX   Telefax: 739.49.75

Iceland – Islande
Mál Mog Menning
Laugavegi 18, Pósthólf 392
121 Reykjavik   Tel. 15199/24240

India – Inde
Oxford Book and Stationery Co.
Scindia House
New Delhi 110001   Tel. 331.5896/5308
Telex: 31 61990 AM IN
Telefax: (11)332.5993
17 Park Street
Calcutta 700016   Tel. 240832

Indonesia – Indonésie
Pdii-Lipi
P.O. Box 269/JKSMG/88
Jakarta 12790   Tel. 583467
Telex: 62 875

Ireland – Irlande
TDC Publishers – Library Suppliers
12 North Frederick Street
Dublin 1   Tel. 744835/749677
Telex: 33530 TDCP EI   Telefax: 748416

Italy – Italie
Libreria Commissionaria Sansoni
Via Benedetto Fortini, 120/10
Casella Post. 552
50125 Firenze   Tel. (055)64.54.15
Telex: 570466   Telefax: (055)64.12.57
Via Bartolini 29
20155 Milano   Tel. 36.50.83
La diffusione delle pubblicazioni OCSE viene assicurata
dalle principali librerie ed anche da:
Editrice e Libreria Herder
Piazza Montecitorio 120
00186 Roma   Tel. 679.46.28
Telex: NATEL I 621427
Libreria Hoepli
Via Hoepli 5
20121 Milano   Tel. 86.54.46
Telex: 31.33.95   Telefax: (02)805.28.86
Libreria Scientifica
Dott. Lucio de Biasio 'Aeiou'
Via Meravigli 16
20123 Milano   Tel. 805.68.98
Telefax: 800175

Japan – Japon
OECD Publications and Information Centre
Landic Akasaka Building
2-3-4 Akasaka, Minato-ku
Tokyo 107   Tel. (81.3)3586.2016
Telefax: (81.3)3584.7929

Korea – Corée
Kyobo Book Centre Co. Ltd.
P.O. Box 1658, Kwang Hwa Moon
Seoul   Tel. (REP)730.78.91
Telefax: 735.0030

Malaysia/Singapore – Malaisie/Singapour
Co-operative Bookshop Ltd.
University of Malaya
P.O. Box 1127, Jalan Pantai Baru
59700 Kuala Lumpur
Malaysia   Tel. 756.5000/756.5425
Telefax: 757.3661
Information Publications Pte. Ltd.
Pei-Fu Industrial Building
24 New Industrial Road No. 02-06
Singapore 1953   Tel. 283.1786/283.1798
Telefax: 284.8875

Netherlands – Pays-Bas
SDU Uitgeverij
Christoffel Plantijnstraat 2
Postbus 20014
2500 EA's-Gravenhage   Tel. (070 3)78.99.11
Voor bestellingen: Tel. (070 3)78.98.80
Telex: 32486 stdru   Telefax: (070 3)47.63.51

New Zealand – Nouvelle-Zélande
GP Publications Ltd.
Customer Services
33 The Esplanade - P.O. Box 38-900
Petone, Wellington
Tel. (04)685-555   Telefax: (04)685-333

Norway – Norvège
Narvesen Info Center - NIC
Bertrand Narvesens vei 2
P.O. Box 6125 Etterstad
0602 Oslo 6   Tel. (02)57.33.00
Telex: 79668 NIC N   Telefax: (02)68.19.01

Pakistan
Mirza Book Agency
65 Shahrah Quaid-E-Azam
Lahore 3   Tel. 66839
Telex: 44886 UBL PK. Attn: MIRZA BK

Portugal
Livraria Portugal
Rua do Carmo 70-74, Apart. 2681
1117 Lisboa Codex   Tel.: 347.49.82/3/4/5
Telefax: (01) 347.02.64

Singapore/Malaysia – Singapour/Malaisie
See Malaysia/Singapore" – Voir «Malaisie/Singapour»

Spain – Espagne
Mundi-Prensa Libros S.A.
Castelló 37, Apartado 1223
Madrid 28001   Tel. (91) 431.33.99
Telex: 49370 MPLI   Telefax: 575.39.98
Libreria Internacional AEDOS
Consejo de Ciento 391
08009 - Barcelona   Tel. (93) 301-86-15
     Telefax: (93) 317-01-41
Llibreria de la Generalitat
Palau Moja, Rambla dels Estudis, 118
08002 - Barcelona   Telefax: (93) 412.18.54
     Tel. (93) 318.80.12 (Subscripcions)
(93) 302.67.23 (Publicacions)

Sri Lanka
Centre for Policy Research
c/o Mercantile Credit Ltd.
55, Janadhipathi Mawatha
Colombo 1   Tel. 438471-9, 440346
Telex: 21138 VAVALEX CE   Telefax: 94.1.448900

Sweden – Suède
Fritzes Fackboksföretaget
Box 16356, Regeringsgatan 12
103 27 Stockholm   Tel. (08)23.89.00
Telex: 12387   Telefax: (08)20.50.21
Subscription Agency/Abonnements:
Wennergren-Williams AB
Nordenflychtsvägen 74, Box 30004
104 25 Stockholm   Tel. (08)13.67.00
Telex: 19937   Telefax: (08)618.62.32

Switzerland – Suisse
OECD Publications and Information Centre
Schedestrasse 7
D-W 5300 Bonn 1 (Germany)   Tel. (49.228)21.60.45
Telefax: (49.228)26.11.04
Librairie Payot
6 rue Grenus
1211 Genève 11   Tel. (022)731.89.50
Telex: 28356
Subscription Agency - Service des Abonnements
Naville S.A.
7, rue Lévrier
1201 Genève   Tél.: (022) 732.24.00
Telefax: (022) 738.48.03
Maditec S.A.
Chemin des Palettes 4
1020 Renens/Lausanne   Tel. (021)635.08.65
Telefax: (021)635.07.80
United Nations Bookshop/Librairie des Nations-Unies
Palais des Nations
1211 Genève 10   Tel. (022)734.14.73
Telex: 412962   Telefax: (022)740.09.31

Taiwan – Formose
Good Faith Worldwide Int'l. Co. Ltd.
9th Floor, No. 118, Sec. 2
Chung Hsiao E. Road
Taipei   Tel. 391.7396/391.7397
Telefax: (02) 394.9176

Thailand – Thaïlande
Suksit Siam Co. Ltd.
1715 Rama IV Road, Samyan
Bangkok 5   Tel. 251.1630

Turkey – Turquie
Kültur Yayinlari Is-Türk Ltd. Sti.
Atatürk Bulvari No. 191/Kat. 21
Kavaklidere/Ankara   Tel. 25.07.60
Dolmabahce Cad. No. 29
Besiktas/Istanbul   Tel. 160.71.88
Telex: 43482B

United Kingdom – Royaume-Uni
HMSO
Gen. enquiries   Tel. (071) 873 0011
Postal orders only:
P.O. Box 276, London SW8 5DT
Personal Callers HMSO Bookshop
49 High Holborn, London WC1V 6HB
Telex: 297138   Telefax: 071 873 2000
Branches at: Belfast, Birmingham, Bristol, Edinburgh,
Manchester

United States – États-Unis
OECD Publications and Information Centre
2001 L Street N.W., Suite 700
Washington, D.C. 20036-4910   Tel. (202)785.6323
Telefax: (202)785.0350

Venezuela
Libreria del Este
Avda F. Miranda 52, Aptdo. 60337, Edificio Galipán
Caracas 106   Tel. 951.1705/951.2307/951.1297
Telegram: Libreste Caracas

Yugoslavia – Yougoslavie
Jugoslovenska Knjiga
Knez Mihajlova 2, P.O. Box 36
Beograd   Tel.: (011)621.992
Telex: 12466 jk bgd   Telefax: (011)625.970

Orders and inquiries from countries where Distributors
have not yet been appointed should be sent to: OECD
Publications Service, 2 rue André-Pascal, 75775 Paris
Cedex 16, France.
Les commandes provenant de pays où l'OCDE n'a pas
encore désigné de distributeur devraient être adressées à :
OCDE, Service des Publications, 2, rue André-Pascal,
75775 Paris Cédex 16, France.

75880-7/91

OECD PUBLICATIONS, 2 rue André-Pascal, 75775 PARIS CEDEX 16
PRINTED IN FRANCE
(97 91 07 1) ISBN 92-64-13584-7 - No. 45697 1991